THE M.I.T. PAPERBACK SERIES

BIOLOGICAL ORDER

KARL TAYLOR COMPTON LECTURES

KARL TAYLOR COMPTON *1887–1954*

The Karl Taylor Compton Lectures honor the memory of the ninth president of the Massachusetts Institute of Technology by bringing to the M.I.T. community some of the great minds of our time who contribute to the integration of scientific, cultural, and philosophical concerns — a synthesis richly achieved by Karl Taylor Compton and shared with colleagues and students during his long leadership of the Institute.

BIOLOGICAL ORDER

by

André Lwoff *, 1902 -*

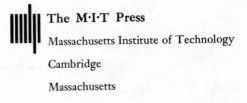

The **M·I·T** Press

Massachusetts Institute of Technology

Cambridge

Massachusetts

QH
349
.L9

First M.I.T. Press Paperback Edition, February 1965

Library of Congress
Catalog Card No. 62–16929

Printed in the
United States of America

PREFACE

A scientist invited to deliver a series of lectures has first to select a theme which is determined essentially by his own field of interest and activity. The scientist then has to organize the lectures according to the interest and knowledge of the potential audience. This is especially important when a biologist is going to lecture in an institute of technology, despite the fact that this institute enjoys an excellent department of biology. The Compton Lectures, as I was told, are intended for a very large group of students, mostly physicists and chemists. After discussing this matter with my M.I.T. colleagues, I decided that these Compton Lectures would be directed toward the young physicists and chemists, with a very specific goal, namely to interest them in biological problems. It is in view of this ambitious aim that biological order was selected as a theme. The lectures, being intended for physicists and chemists, were planned as if the audience knew nothing about biology. I certainly have to apologize for this hypothesis.

Thus life, the organism, and the cell have been defined and the problem of biological order posed in its generality. We have discussed in succession: the hereditary order, namely the nature, structure, reproduction, and variation of the genetic material; the functional order, namely the control of enzyme synthesis, and the interaction of heredity and environment; and finally viruses as representative of a specific order and at the same time of disorder. Biological order has been considered at the molecular level in its static as well as in its dynamic aspects. I have tried to explain how molecules communicate and interact, and how the organism controls and adjusts its molecular balance.

May I express the hope that the reader, after having penetrated into the molecular intimacy of the living being, will be left with the impression that biological order, the foundation of biology, is a fascinating subject.

ANDRÉ LWOFF

Paris
May, 1960

CONTENTS

BIOLOGICAL ORDER

I. INTRODUCTION TO BIOLOGY

Life

Biology is, by etymology, the study of life. Life is difficult to define, and the easiest solution is to decide, as so many people have done, that its definition is impossible. In his book *The Nature of Life*, Szent-Györgyi writes: "Life as such does not exist; nobody has ever seen it. . . . The noun 'life' has no sense, there being no such thing." Yet, it is well known that definition is among the methods for discovery. It is, as a matter of fact, an excellent heuristic method. For it obliges one to condense the essential of a category or of a phenomenon into a formula — the formula containing everything it has to contain, and excluding everything it has to exclude. To cast a good definition is therefore useful, for this exercise compels critical consideration of all the terms or aspects of a problem.

Life may be considered either as a *property*, or as a *manifestation*, or as a *state* of organisms. This might or might not satisfy the biologist. The physicist will immediately ask two questions: (1) What is an organism? (2) What is the specific property of living organisms that does not exist in the inanimate world and is therefore characteristic of life?

The Organism

An organism may be visualized as a complex, organized, specific system able to reproduce its kind. An organism never appears *de novo* but always derives from a pre-existing, identical organism.

Biological systems — that is, organisms — are endowed with genetic continuity.

The organism synthesizes its constitutive parts. Syntheses can take place only if the system is provided with food and energy, which are consumed in the processes involved; this is metabolism. When provided with food, the organism metabolizes, grows, and reproduces. The organism is the independent unit of reproduction.

An organism is composed essentially of macromolecular compounds, among which are nucleic acids and proteins. Even the smallest organism contains a few thousand different species of macromolecules. The simplest organism is therefore a relatively complex machine. All known complex systems which contain macromolecules and are able to reproduce their kind belong to the living systems. Reproduction of a complex system containing macromolecules is therefore characteristic of life. And such a complex, independent unit of integrated structures and functions that reproduces true to type can only be an organism, a living organism.

These statements might be considered too factual, and some would perhaps prefer a more original and sophisticated definition. The formulation which follows is an attempt at a summary of the views expressed by Norbert Wiener, in his fascinating book *Cybernetics:* "Living organisms are metastable Maxwell demons whose stable state is to be dead."

The Cell and Organisms

Organisms belong to two categories: (*a*) the protists or microbes, which are composed of one cell and are therefore the lower organisms; (*b*) those which are composed of many cells, the so-called higher organisms, the group to which we are so proud to belong.

In 1857, Leydig described and defined the cell as a mass of protoplasm containing a nucleus. This is an excellent definition. Let us consider, for example, a microbial cell, a bacterium. It is a sphere about 1 μ in diameter. When properly handled and stained, it shows a dark central body, the nucleus, surrounded by a pale substance called cytoplasm.

The cells of a multicellular organism are specialized, that is, differentiated. The liver cells are different from the kidney cells and from the brain cells. The differentiated cells are organized into tissues and the tissues into organs. The functioning of each cell is controlled by the organism as a whole. The cells of a multicellular organism are the integrated, dependent, and interdependent parts of the organism. In this way, cells of a multicellular organism differ from the microbial cell which is an organism itself, an *independent system of reproduction*. One category, the cells of an organism, corresponds to parts of an organism; the other, the microbial cell, to a complete organism.

Organisms contain macromolecules endowed with a specific structure and a specific function. In order that life can be perpetuated, these macromolecules have to work in co-operation. The smallest unit of integration, co-operation, and reproduction is the cell. Both the cell of a multicellular organism and the microbe are the ultimate units of integration and reproduction. As such, they share so many essential features that the common traits have transcended the differences. The term *cell* is now used for the metazoal cell as well as for the microbe. But it is essential to know that the word *cell* applies to two different categories of systems: the dependent part of the multicellular organism and the independent unicellular organism.

Life, Organism, Reproduction, and Assimilation

Assimilation is sometimes listed among the discriminative features of life. From a biochemical point of view, assimilation, "the action of making like," is the assemblage of small building blocks — amino acids or nucleic bases — common to all living beings, into specific macromolecules — proteins or nucleic acids — that are characteristic for each species. Assimilation is essentially the organization of complex specific sequences. Assimilation is a patternization.

Only a living being is able to synthesize a few thousand specific macromolecules, putting each of the twenty amino acids and each of the four nucleic bases where it belongs. This can be accomplished only because of the presence and activity of specific templates that are parts of the living system.

BIOLOGICAL ORDER

The formula "the living being reproduces its kind" expresses the fact that each organism produces its own specific macromolecules. Metabolism is a prerequisite for assimilation. In the last analysis, assimilation precludes and includes metabolism, and the interplay of specific structures and functions. It corresponds, at the molecular level as well as at the level of the organism, to synthesis, growth, and reproduction true to type and to genetic continuity. In this sense, assimilation is certainly a discriminative feature of life. Assimilation is correlative to life, and life is correlative to assimilation. As a matter of fact, an organism can reproduce only if it is endowed with the power to assimilate. Reproduction includes assimilation. But the words *reproduction* and *assimilation* will take their full significance only when something has been learned concerning biological specificity. Anyhow, the notions of life, organism, reproduction, and assimilation cannot be separated.

REFERENCES

Brachet, J., and Mirsky, A. E., eds. (1959). *The Cell.— Biochemistry, Physiology, Morphology*. Academic Press, New York and London.
Dobell, C. C. (1911). The principles of protistology. *Arch. Protistenk., 23,* 269–310.
Dobell, C. C. (1932). *Antony van Leeuwenhoek and His "Little Animals."* John Bale, Sons & Danielsson, London.
McElroy, W. D., and Glass, B., eds. (1957). *A Symposium on the Chemical Basis of Heredity*. The Johns Hopkins Press, Baltimore.
Schrödinger, E. (1944). *What Is Life? The Physical Aspect of the Living Cell.* The University Press, Cambridge.
Stanier, R. Y., Doudoroff, M., and Adelberg, E. A. (1957). *The Microbial World*. Prentice-Hall, Inc., Englewood Cliffs, N. J.
Szent-Györgyi, A. (1948). *Nature of Life*. Academic Press, New York.

II. THE PROBLEMS

Organism and Molecules

A bacterium, which is a microorganism, absorbs food, metabolizes, grows, and divides; two bacteria are thus produced out of one. This process is called reproduction by binary fission. But we are not interested in the external appearance of things. We are not interested in what we see but in what we do not see, in the invisible essence of things.

A molecule is the smallest unit quantity of matter which can exist by itself and retain all the properties of the original substance. A molecule can be split into fragments, but each fragment is necessarily different from the original structure. Molecules might aggregate, but a molecule cannot divide. Neither can a molecule grow. Thus the growth and division of a bacterium is not the growth and division of its molecules. What is reproduction at the molecular level?

The living world is composed of thousands of species differing in their size, shape, chemical composition, nutrition, metabolism, etc. But all these species are constructed with the same building blocks. The specificity of an organism in the last analysis is, and can only be, the consequence of the specific structure of its macromolecules. This means that each individual always produces identical macromolecules. What is biological specificity? How is the information stored which is responsible for the biological specificity and diversity? How is it reproduced?

Everybody knows that organisms undergo variations, some of which are inheritable. This is the basis of evolution. The statement that an organism reproduces true to type is therefore true only statistically. Heredity and variation are combined in the living system. The structure of the organism includes its past, its historical experience. What is the molecular basis of hereditary variation?

An organism is an integrated unit of structure and functions. In an organism, all molecules have to work in harmony. Each molecule has to know what the other molecules are doing. Each molecule must be able to receive messages and must be disciplined enough to obey orders. How has the organism solved the problem of inter-molecular communication?

An organism rarely lives in a constant environment. When the environment varies, the organism has to cope with the variations. As a matter of fact, the constitutive, dependent parts of the organism, its molecules, are submitted to a dual action: they are controlled by the genetic material, which is responsible for heredity and evolution, and at the same time they are subject to the action of the environment. And one would like to know something about the interaction of hereditary and environmental factors, about the way the organism as a whole decides what it has to do when faced with a given situation.

Everyone knows that things are not always as they should be. This is in a sense fortunate, for otherwise life would be boring; I mean, of course, molecular life. Freedom is essential for the development and blooming of the human being. But as part of an organized society the human being has to accept a certain number of restraints. This is true for molecules. When a molecule develops a strong personality and refuses to submit herself to the common rule, the organism is dangerously threatened. In an ideal molecular society, each molecule works for the community, that is, for the organism. This is what happens normally. Yet a molecule sometimes decides to get rid of the shackles of co-ordination and to work for its own profit. As a result, all sorts of molecular diseases are produced. Molecular freedom is a catastrophe. Molecular diseases, of which viral diseases are only one aspect, pose a number of problems that we shall have to discuss.

The Subject

Our subject is biological order, and the word *order* has hardly been pronounced. As everyone knows, order is the fixed arrangement present in the existing constitution of things. Order may also be considered as a sequence or succession in space or time. Biological order is all that, and it is especially a sequence in space *and* time. Biological order is dual, structural and functional, static and dynamic. Structural and functional orders are the complementary aspects of the living being. A living being is a dual system of order. We have to know what this dual system is.

Metabolism

A bacterium is seeded in a proper nutrient medium. Food is taken in. Chemical reactions are performed. Syntheses take place. This is metabolism.

Today, almost everything is known concerning the synthesis of the building blocks, or intermediary metabolism. One atom is attached to another, a molecule is methylated, carboxylated, or aminated (attachment of, respectively, a —CH$_3$, a —COOH, or an —NH$_2$ group), and finally each atom is exactly where it belongs. The synthesis of each building block is a stepwise process. As an example, the biosynthesis of the amino acid tryptophan is depicted in Figure 20. In order to synthesize tryptophan, each reaction has to be catalyzed by a specific enzyme. Enzymes are specific proteins. Some proteins have an enzymatic activity by themselves. Other enzymes work only with the help of a specific coenzyme. Most of the enzymes can be extracted from the cell and purified. It was thus learned that a given enzyme performs only one chemical reaction.

In a biosynthetic chain of reactions, each reaction requires energy. The energy needed for the syntheses is provided by the oxidation of food, for example sugar. The organism "burns" sugar, and the energy obtained is stored as high-energy bonds, for example in the form of adenosine triphosphoric acid. The oxidation of food and the storage of energy involve a series of chemical reactions, each one again mediated by a specific enzyme.

As a result of the functioning of the enzymes, the bacterium synthesizes more enzymes, and its size increases. The nucleus divides, and finally the bacterium itself divides, thus giving rise to two daughter cells.

Simplicity or Complexity

A few years ago a well-known physical chemist interested in bacterial physiology wrote this remarkable sentence, "The structure of the bacterial cell is simple." This is true of course from the bacterial point of view. The bacterial machine works, synthesizes, grows, and divides. And, as the bacterium is devoid of brain, it has no problems. But for us, the suffering human beings who try to penetrate the intimate nature of life, the bacterial cell, despite being small, is far from simple. In this machine of around 1 μ diameter,* corresponding to a volume of 10^{-12} milliliter,† a few thousand specific molecular species are at work, manufacturing more of their specific kind. And we would rather be inclined to say with Antony van Leeuwenhoek, who in 1676 discovered the bacterial world, "Dear God, what marvels there are in so small a creature."

The fact that life could *not* be something simple has been suspected for almost a century. In his famed classical book, *Les phénomènes de la vie communs aux animaux et aux plantes* (*The Phenomena of Life Common to Animals and Plants*), Claude Bernard produced an impressive statement. "The formula $C_{18}H_9NO_2$," he wrote, "by which one attempts to describe the protoplasm, is illusive. In fact, the protoplasm is much more complicated." This was, around 1875, the state of our knowledge, or perhaps the state of our ignorance. It should, however, not be concluded that knowledge and ignorance are synonymous. Anyhow, Claude Bernard certainly had no idea of how much more complicated protoplasm really is.

Unity

At first sight, the problem seems formidable and the situation hopeless. A cell contains some 2,000 to 5,000 species of macromole-

---

* 1 μ is one thousandth part of a millimeter.

† If they were cubes, 10^{12} of them, that is, a thousand billions, could be packed into 1 milliliter.

cules. Moreover, nature has produced an immense variety of categories of different organisms. Yet, when the living world is considered at the cellular level, one discovers unity. *Unity of plan:* each cell possesses a nucleus imbedded in protoplasm. *Unity of function:* the metabolism is essentially the same in each cell. *Unity of composition:* the main macromolecules of all living beings are composed of the same small molecules. For, in order to build the immense diversity of the living systems, nature has made use of a strictly limited number of building blocks. The problem of diversity of structures and functions, the problem of heredity, and the problem of diversification of species have been solved by the elegant use of a small number of building blocks organized into specific macromolecules.

What specificity is will be learned later. For the time being, it is only necessary to know that the most important macromolecules are nucleic acids and proteins. Nucleic acids are made of four nucleic

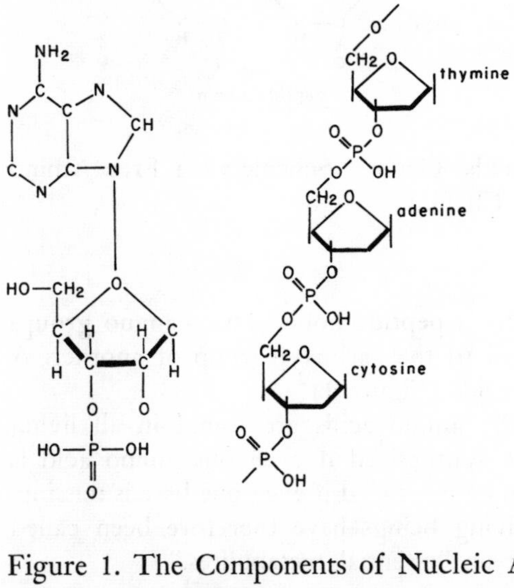

Figure 1. The Components of Nucleic Acid.

(*a*) Adenosine-3-phosphate (nucleotide): adenine, ribose, phosphoric acid.
(*b*) Fragment of a nucleic acid chain. The pentoses of the nucleotides are united by phosphodiester bonds.

bases, each bound to a sugar to form a nucleoside. A molecule of phosphoric acid is attached to each sugar, thus forming a nucleotide. The nucleotides are united by phosphodiester bonds, thus forming a long chain (Figure 1).

The analysis of proteins reveals that they are composed of twenty amino acids. An amino acid is, as indicated by its name, an aminated acid. Glycine, for example, is aminated acetic acid. In proteins,

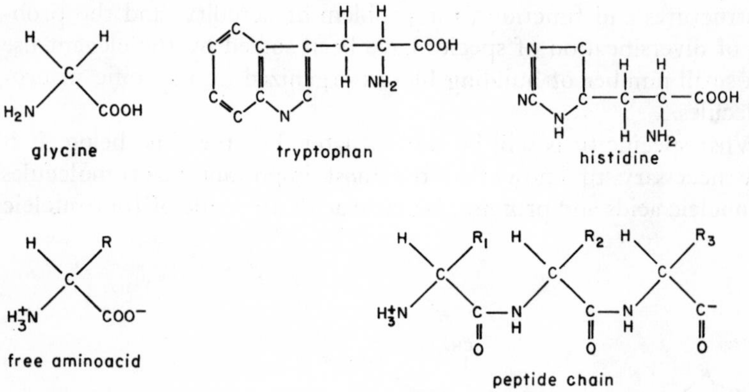

glycine   tryptophan   histidine

free aminoacid   peptide chain

Figure 2. Three Amino Acids, General Scheme of a Free Amino Acid, Scheme of a Peptide Chain.

amino acids are assembled by a peptide bond. The α-amino groups of one amino acid are joined to the carboxyl group of another. A protein is a chain of amino acids (Figure 2).

The nucleic bases and the amino acids are found in all living beings. No proteins can be synthesized if even one amino acid is missing. No nucleic acid can be produced if even one base is missing. These necessary cogs of living beings have therefore been called "fundamental constituents" or "essential metabolites."

Thus the microorganism is a complex system built of a few building blocks assembled into specific macromolecules. Each macromolecule is endowed with a specific function. The machine is built for doing precisely what it does. We may admire it, but we should not lose our heads. If the living system did not perform its task, it would not exist. We have simply to learn how it performs its task.

III.

THE HEREDITARY ORDER:
GENETIC INFORMATION

Birth of the Modern Concept

In the year 1835, Hegel published his well-known *Esthetic*. I have a suspicion that a small fraction of the students here could be somewhat unfamiliar with Hegel's *Esthetic*. Whatever the case may be, in this fundamental book, among a number of irrelevant remarks, irrelevant for us today, the problem of life is pertinently discussed.

The tree is a living reality, says the German philosopher. In its germ the determinants exist as potentialities. Nothing is in the tree which was not already in the germ, and yet in the germ one does not see anything, even with the microscope. We can visualize the determinants as existing in the germ as extremely simple forces.

In 1864, the British philosopher Herbert Spencer, in his *Principles of Biology*, stated that in every organism the total of hereditary properties is determined by distinct physiological units which are formed by the assemblage of chemical units into immensely complex compounds. Yet the most extraordinary biological intuition was that of a physicist, Schrödinger. Starting from small molecules — wrote Schrödinger in 1944 — it is possible to build large aggregates without the dull device of repetition. In a complicated organic molecule, every stone, every group of atoms, plays an individual role not entirely equivalent to that of the others. The atoms forming a molecule are united by forces of exactly the same nature as the numerous atoms which build a true solid, a crystal. The most essential part of a living being, the chromosomal fiber, presenting the same solidity of structure as a crystal, may be called an aperiodic crystal. Schrödinger adds that we believe the whole chromosomal fiber to be an aperiodic solid.

Chromosomes have been known to cytologists for a long time. They are relatively large and easy to stain, and they stain heavily — hence their name, which means "colored bodies."

As early as 1866, Haeckel realized that the nucleus, which contains the chromosomes, is the cellular organelle which is responsible for the maintenance and transmission of the inheritable characters. And Weismann, in 1892, understood that the inheritable characters were located in the chromosome. The chromosome, according to Weismann, is composed of spherical bodies, or *ides*. Each ide contains determinants, and each determinant is composed of *biophores*, which all represent a different character. The biophore corresponds to the actual gene, that is, to the unit of genetic material, the unit of biological order.

The quantitative study of the transmission of hereditary characters had been started in 1865 by Gregor Mendel. But Mendel's laws remained ignored until, in 1900, they were rediscovered independently by Hugo de Vries, Correns, and Tschermak. This was the beginning of formal genetics. Each gene was assigned a specific place on the chromosome. But it was not until 1944 that the genetic material was identified chemically, and not until 1953 that its structure was disclosed.

The living being — the organism, the unit of life — has been defined as an independent system of integrated structures and functions. It is a highly complex system, able to reproduce its kind, that is, to multiply the specific biological order. What is the molecular basis of biological order and specificity? How is order stored in the organism? If a molecule is unable to divide, how is a molecule of hereditary material reproduced?

Necessity of Variation

The statement that the organism reproduces its kind is of course true, but only statistically true. If the primitive living being had always given birth to an identical system, life would probably have disappeared long ago as the result of the drastic changes undergone by the primary environment. Living beings, as highly improbable systems, can only be the result of a stepwise process, which is evolution. Evolution is the sum of the alterations which have taken place between the beginning, or let us say an initial primitive state, and a given, later, present state, which I would dislike to call final.

It is admitted that the essential cause of evolutionary variation has been the gene mutation, which is a sudden, hereditary change. Mutations still take place nowadays. It is, I suppose, quite obvious that if all individuals belonging to one species were, and would remain, identical, there would be no such thing as genetics. So it is most fortunate that mutations do exist. In the absence of mutations, it would be difficult to understand heredity. The principles of genetics are based on the study of differences, of transmissible differences.

For example, a plant producing red flowers may give rise to modified offspring, or mutants, producing white flowers. Or a bacterium synthesizing the amino acid tryptophan gives rise to offspring unable to synthesize tryptophan. Each time such situations are analyzed, it is found that the gene mutation, or the hereditary change, corresponds to an alteration of an enzymatic system. This is the Beadle–Tatum law: one gene controls the synthesis of one enzyme. Each enzyme corresponds to a specific gene. As a result of a mutation, the ability to synthesize a given enzyme, a given specific catalyst, is acquired or is lost. And the change is hereditary, that is, transmitted to the offspring.

Let us give a few concrete examples. The original, the so-called wild type, of a given bacterium is able to synthesize the enzyme β-galactosidase, which splits lactose into glucose and galactose. But it may give rise to mutants devoid of this enzyme.

The wild type of another bacterium synthesizes the amino acid methionine. The biosynthesis is mediated by a series of enzymes, each responsible for a given step in the sequence of reactions. Here again, the bacterium may produce mutants unable to synthesize methionine. When examined, it is found that one of the enzymes responsible for the stepwise synthesis is missing.

Human beings normally oxidize the amino acid phenylalanine. Some human beings, some human mutants, are unable to oxidize this amino acid by the normal route. As a consequence, phenylpyruvic acid appears in the urine. The I.Q. of these persons is generally lower than 10. They are idiots, unable to think. This is, however, not important in this analysis. What is important is that the enzyme present in normal human beings and responsible for the normal pathway of phenylalanine is missing in the phenylpyruvic idiots.

Long before the specific alteration responsible for a mutation had been chemically known, and long before the specific responsible enzyme had been identified, the site of the biological alteration, as already stated, had been located on the chromosome. The responsible chromosomal structures were called *genes* and described as units of variation.

The problem was of course to identify the substrate of the hereditary variation, that is, to identify the nature of the entity controlling the production of an enzyme. This was accomplished by the study of bacteria.

The Genetic Material Identified

TRANSFORMATION. Many bacteria possess an outer layer, or capsule, which is a specific polysaccharide. The agent of pneumonia, the *Pneumococcus*, exhibits many varieties or types. The capsule of each of them is built of a specific polysaccharide in which the nature of the glucidic subunits are different. The polysaccharides are easy to identify, for a polysaccharide injected into an animal elicits the formation of a specific protein called an antibody (Figure 3). An anti-III-antibody combines specifically with the polysaccharide III and not with polysaccharide II. It agglutinates bacteria of type III and not of type II.

Sometimes, as a result of a sudden change, a mutation, a *Pneumococcus* loses the ability to produce its specific polysaccharide. When this capsuleless, polysaccharideless bacterium, originally of type II, for example, is grown in the presence of extracts of type III bacteria, one recovers capsulated bacteria of type III. Something present in the extract of type III bacteria has *transformed* a capsuleless, originally type II bacterium into a capsulated type III. The extract of type III contains the "information" for the synthesis of type III polysaccharide, and this information can be transferred to a bac-

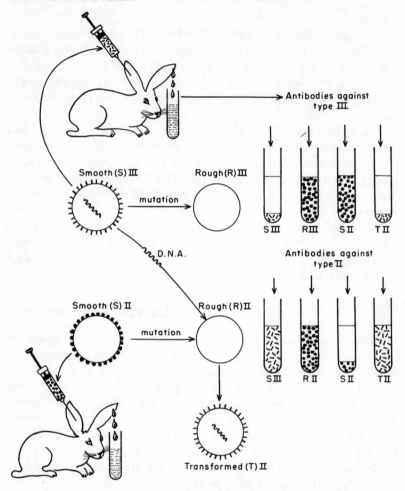

Figure 3. Transformation of *Pneumococcus* and the Transforming Principle.

The smooth (S) *Pneumococcus* type III gives off rough (R) mutants devoid of capsule, that is, of the specific polysaccharide characteristic of the type. The smooth *Pneumococcus* type II also gives off rough mutants. The DNA extracted from type III transforms the rough, originally II, into a smooth bacterium possessing the polysaccharide of type III.

The antibodies against type III agglutinate the smooth III and the transformed II but not the rough strains III and II.

The antibodies against type II agglutinate the smooth II but not the smooth III, the rough II, and the transformed II.

terium that was originally type II. This information was called the "transforming principle." This principle could not be metaphysical; it had to be an organic molecule.

The bacterial extract containing the transforming principle was fractionated. Each fraction was tested for its transforming ability. Finally, in 1944, Avery, MacLeod, and McCarthy succeeded in obtaining a pure active substance that was identified as desoxyribonucleic acid, or DNA.

Once a bacterium has been "transformed" by a specific DNA, it gives rise to transformed offspring. The daughter bacteria have inherited the specific information. They duplicate it in turn. From them, a transforming principle can be extracted again. Thus the transforming principle, the specific nucleic acid controlling the synthesis of a specific substance, is multiplied and regularly transmitted from cell to cell. But this specific nucleic acid is not directly responsible for the synthesis of the polysaccharide. When it is present, the bacterium produces a specific enzyme that can perform a specific reaction, in this case the synthesis of a specific polysaccharide.

This is not a unique case but one particular example of a general phenomenon. Many bacteria have been transformed with DNA coming from a closely related form. In all the cases of transformation studied so far, the introduction of the desoxyribonucleic acid of the donor bacterium into the recipient organism endows it with the capacity to synthesize a given enzyme, that is, endows it with a given physiological potentiality. This conclusion has been confirmed and extended by the study of viruses. The nucleic acid of viruses can be separated from the protein components. When a pure, naked, specific viral nucleic acid penetrates a cell, specific viral proteins and specific viral infectious particles are produced. The nucleic acid of viruses plays the same role in heredity as the nucleic acid of bacteria: both control the synthesis of specific proteins.

Structure of the Genetic Material

DESOXYRIBONUCLEIC ACID. Desoxyribonucleic acid, or DNA, contains three types of molecules: (*a*) purine and pyrimidine bases, (*b*) a pentose, desoxyribose, and (*c*) phosphoric acid.

The two purine bases, adenine and guanine, and the two pyrimidine bases, thymine and cytosine, are represented in Figure 4. Each base is attached to a molecule of desoxyribose in position 1 carrying a phosphorus in position 3. This is a unit, a desoxyribonucleotide (Figure 1). In the nucleic acid, nucleotides are linked by phosphodiester bonds. The result is a long chain. (See also Figure 1.)

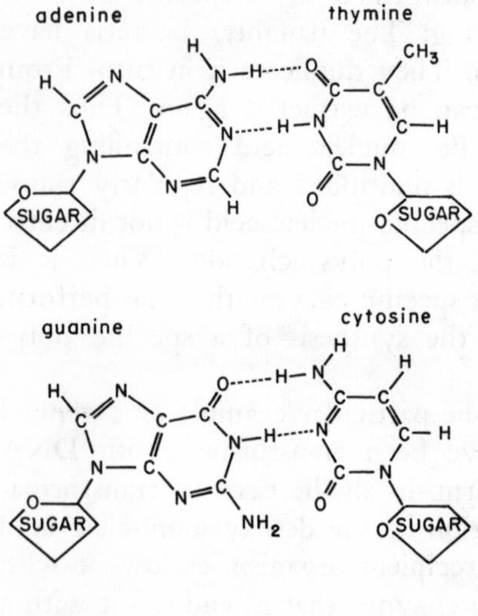

Figure 4. The Four Nucleic Bases in the Desoxyribonucleic Acid.

Each pyrimidine base is bound to a purine base by hydrogen bonds. Adenine is bound to thymine, guanine to cytosine.

Thanks to James Watson and Francis Crick, the structure of DNA has been disclosed. DNA is a double polynucleotide chain. The two chains are held together by hydrogen bonds between the bases. A pyrimidine base is bound to a purine base: adenine to thymine, guanine to cytosine. Thus in the double DNA helix, the ratio of adenine/thymine and of guanine/cytosine is equal to 1. The two chains run in opposite directions. They are twined around each other (Figure 5).

This structure is now firmly established. The evidence derives from X-ray studies as well as from physical chemical data (titration curves, light scattering, viscosity, sedimentation, kinetics of breakdown by gamma rays and enzymes).

Thus desoxyribonucleic acid is a double helix. Each helical chain is made up of a chain of desoxyribose phosphate with one base attached to each sugar.

RIBONUCLEIC ACID. DNA is the genetic material of all animals, plants, microorganisms, and of some viruses. But in a few viruses the genetic material is ribonucleic acid. Ribonucleic acid, or RNA, has the same fundamental structure as DNA: it is a long chain of nucleotides. But whereas the sugar in DNA is desoxyribose, it is ribose in RNA. Moreover, the pyrimidine base thymine present in DNA is, in RNA, replaced by uracil. Finally, whereas DNA is a double helix, RNA is a single helix.

The two nucleic acids, DNA and RNA, both carry genetic information. The substrate of genetic information can only be a feature shared by these two nucleic acids. The common singularity is obviously the linear arrangement of nucleic bases.

The chemical identification of the genetic material by Avery, MacLeod, and McCarthy has been the great discovery of modern biology. It was soon followed by another great discovery, that of the molecular structure of the desoxyribonucleic acid, the Watson–Crick double helix. Both discoveries catalyzed the extraordinary development of genetics, cell physiology, cell biochemistry, and virology, which have now merged into a new integrative discipline: molecular biology.

Figure 5. The Watson-Crick Model
of the DNA Double Helix.

The two chains run in opposite directions. The backbones are constituted by desoxyribose molecules united by phosphodiester bonds. The nucleic bases of one chain are united to the bases of the other chain by hydrogen bonds.

The Molecular Basis
of Enzymatic Specificity

Enzymes are proteins. Proteins are composed of twenty species of amino acids (Figure 6). If, in two protein molecules, these twenty species are organized into one and the same sequence, the two

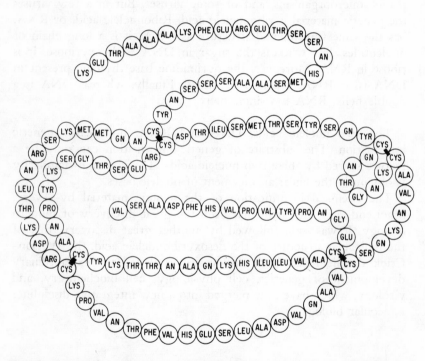

Figure 6. The Molecule of Ribonuclease (from C. B. Anfinsen, *The Molecular Basis of Evolution*).

molecules are necessarily identical. The polypeptide chain of a protein is folded, but it will be admitted that folding depends on the sequence of amino acids and that two identical polypeptide chains are necessarily folded in the same way. Thus, differences in proteins can be due only to differences in the sequence of amino acids which constitute the polypeptide chain, and of course in the proportion of each of the twenty molecular species. Many molecules of the same amino acid may be present in a given protein. A given amino acid, except the terminal one, is necessarily associated to its left and to its right with another amino acid, thus forming a tripeptide (Figure 7). A long polypeptidic chain can be arbitrarily subdivided

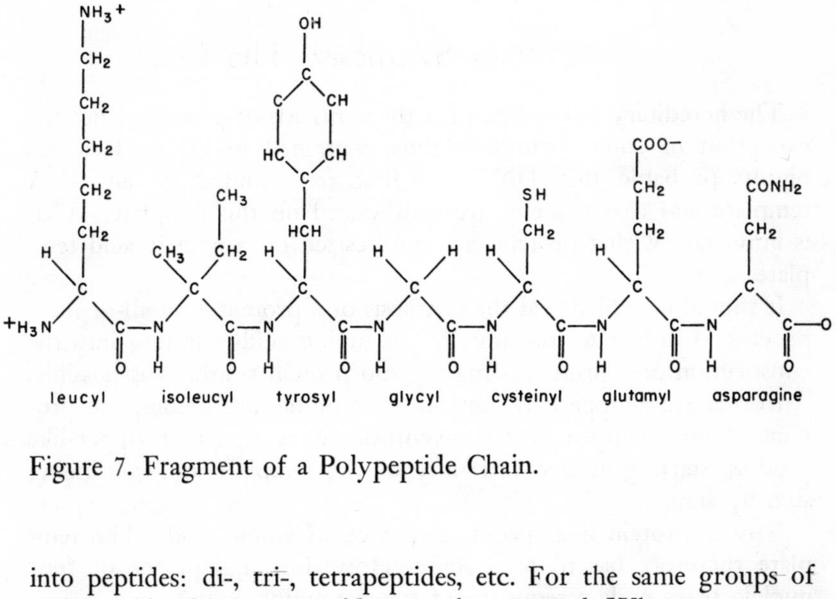

Figure 7. Fragment of a Polypeptide Chain.

into peptides: di-, tri-, tetrapeptides, etc. For the same groups of amino acids, the same peptides may be repeated. When an enzyme acts, the substrate is attached at a specific site, at a specific peptide of the protein. But this specific peptide, if isolated from the rest of the molecule, would not be enzymatically active. In a protein, no individual function can be assigned to any isolated amino acid or group of amino acids. Their functional value depends on the sequence of all amino acids. The unit of function is the whole protein molecule. Each enzyme, being a specific molecule, is necessarily unique. This does not mean that in different species the same enzymatic function cannot be performed by different proteins. The enzyme β-galactosidase, for example, is antigenically (structurally) different in bacteria, in yeasts, and in animals. One problem, the hydrolysis of the β-galactosidic link, has many solutions. The statement that each enzyme is unique applies only to the structure of a given enzyme of a given species, or group of closely related species.

Thus, with twenty different species of amino acids present in various numbers and proportions, a practically infinite array of specific proteins can be synthesized. A given organism, however, synthesizes only a limited number of proteins.

Protein Synthesis: The Code

The hereditary information for the synthesis of proteins, with the exception of some viruses, is thus contained in DNA. It seems highly probable that DNA has first to manufacture an RNA template and that proteins are synthesized on this template. What is important is that proteins are synthesized on a nucleic acid template.

It should be added that the synthesis of a protein is an all-or-none process. If only one, any one, of the amino acids entering into the constitution of a protein is missing, no protein synthesis is possible. An organism is apparently unable to manufacture incomplete proteins. Things happen as if the synthesis were a sort of zipper-like process, starting at one extremity of the template and continuing step by step.

Now a protein is a specific sequence of amino acids. The template therefore has to be specific. How does a sequence of four nucleic bases code a sequence of twenty amino acids?

The problem of the code has been often discussed in recent years. We shall closely follow Francis Crick's excellent review. If just a pair of bases were enough to take care of one amino acid, the number of permutations would be 16, and that is too low. If three bases were required and if any set of three bases could take care of one amino acid, the number of permutations would be 64. Let us consider a sequence of nucleic bases: A C̅ B̅ D A C D B C A D C C B A C. If we assume that the process does not start at the end, how do the amino acids know which template to read? If there is no overlapping, the process can start in A or in C or in B, and the end results will be determined by the point of departure. Moreover, there are 64 permutations. If there is a possible overlapping, the difficulties are the same. Crick, Griffith, and Orgel have worked out a code possessing the following properties:

1. A given amino acid can be coded only on one triplet.
2. A given triplet corresponds to only one amino acid, the total number of "good triplets" being twenty.

This means that 44 triplets out of 64 do not make sense. The good triplets — which make sense — are represented in Figure 8. All the

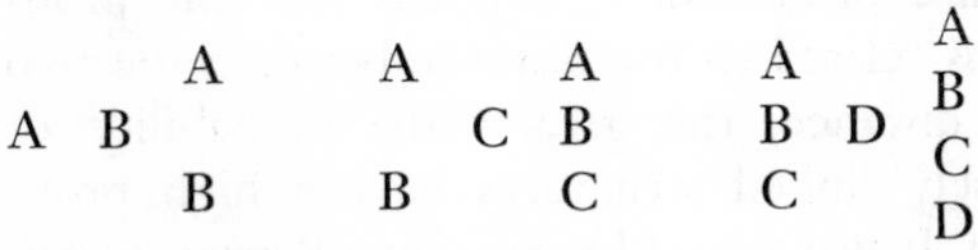

<pre>
        A   A   A   A   A
                                        B
A   B   C   B   B   D   C
        B   B   C   C   D
</pre>

Figure 8. Crick's Tentative Solution of the Coding Problem.

Any combination ABA, ABB, ACB, BCA, etc., is valid. Any other does not make sense.

others are bad triplets. No good triplets can be obtained by combining the adjacent bases of two good triplets. Thus no overlapping is possible. A given sequence of bases necessarily gives rise to a given sequence of amino acids. In this hypothesis, the template is a single chain. The possibility that a protein may be synthesized directly on DNA is not excluded. But the double DNA helix is built from two complementary chains. If one is composed exclusively of "good" triplets, the other chain would necessarily have a large fraction of "bad" triplets and would therefore not make sense. If proteins were synthesized on a DNA template, it would therefore be, according to the discussed code, on one of the chains only.

Finally, the ratio (adenine + thymine)/(guanine + cytosine) varies with the bacterial species from 0.6 to 2.8. How this is reflected in the constitution of enzymes is not yet known.

Anyhow, for the time being, the coding problem is considered as entirely open.*

Mutation

THE NUCLEIC ACID. Thus: (*a*) the genetic information is contained in the nucleic acid; (*b*) the code is a sequence of nucleic bases. Moreover, it has been learned that the nucleic acid is the substrate of mutations, that is, of hereditary variation. The smallest unit of gene variation can be measured by recombination experiments. When two different chromosomes multiply in the same cytoplasm, they mate, and recombinants are produced. It happens that the probability of recombinations is related to the distance between the two factors. The longer the distance, the greater the probability of recombination. Two closely linked structures have a high probability of remaining joined. It was found by Seymour Benzer, working with bacteriophage, that the unit of variation was of the order of three to five nucleotides.

By the use of mutagenic agents, even more refined data were obtained. The spontaneous mutation rate in a bacterium or in a bac-

---

* Since the Compton Lectures were delivered (March, 1960), our knowledge concerning the synthesis of proteins in general and the code in particular has increased considerably.

a. It has been learned that the structural gene, the specific DNA template carrying the genetic information for the synthesis of a given protein, produces a specific RNA "messenger." This messenger, detached from the chromosome, becomes attached onto a nonspecific cytoplasmic ribosome. It is the system ribosome + messenger which assembles the amino acids into a given sequence: diataxy (etymologically, to put in order), thus producing a specific protein. See Jacob and Monod: "Genetic regulatory mechanisms in the synthesis of proteins," *J. Mol. Biol.* (1961), *3*, 318–356; and Jacob and Wollman: *Sexuality and the Genetics of Bacteria,* Academic Press, New York, 1961.

b. The code is now being deciphered: a synthetic poly-uridylic acid contains the information for the synthesis of a protein having the characteristics of poly-L-phenylalanine. A synthetic poly-cytydilic acid takes care of L-proline [M. W. Nirenberg and J. H. Matthaei, *Proc. Nat. Acad. Sci.* (1961), *47*, 1588–1602]. Whether a sequence of three or four nucleotides is involved is not yet known. It is clear, however, that the whole code will soon be deciphered.

teriophage is relatively low: one over one hundred thousand (10^{-5}) to one over one hundred million (10^{-8}) per generation. Many agents are known to increase the probability of mutation. Among these "mutagenic agents" are X rays, ultraviolet rays, and various chemicals, such as nitrogen mustard, organic peroxides, and nitrous acid. When, for example, bacteria, or bacteriophage, or plant viruses, or animal viruses, or naked viral nucleic acid are exposed to nitrous acid, mutants are produced. The kinetics of the process reveals that induction of mutations is a one-hit process. Nitrous acid, when acting on nucleic acid, deaminates nucleic bases, that is, takes off their NH_2 group. This means that the deamination of one base is enough to produce one mutation.

Let us consider, for example, an adenine/thymine pair. As a result of deamination, adenine is transformed into hypoxanthine (Figure 9). The replication of the DNA double helix, as will be seen later,

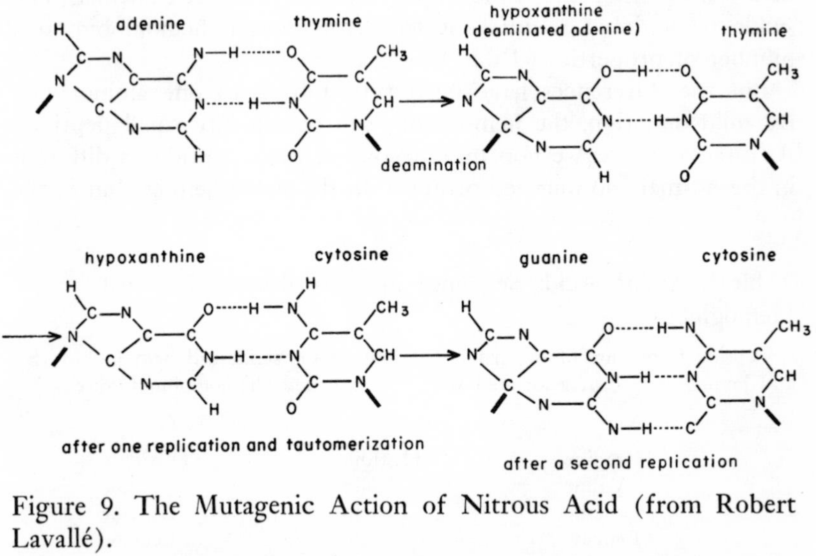

Figure 9. The Mutagenic Action of Nitrous Acid (from Robert Lavallé).

Nitrous acid deaminates adenine, which is thus converted into hypoxanthine. At the first replication, hypoxanthine binds cytosine. At the second replication, cytosine pairs with guanine.

The original base pair adenine/thymine has been replaced by the base pair guanine/cytosine as a result of the action of the nitrous acid.

is essentially the formation, by each of the strands, of a complementary strand. The new base, hypoxanthine, will bind cytosine, which in turn will bind guanine. Thus, as a consequence of a deamination by nitrous acid, the original base pair, adenine/thymine, is in one of the daughter helices, replaced by the pair guanine/cytosine. A gene mutation, in fact a so-called "point mutation," is nothing more.

THE "MUTATED" PROTEIN. We have learned that nucleic acid controls protein synthesis. What is the result of a gene mutation in the protein? What is the difference between the proteins corresponding, respectively, to a given wild-type gene and to this gene once it has undergone a mutation? Hemoglobin, the protein of the red blood cells responsible for the transfer of oxygen, has been the subject of extensive studies. The normal human red cell is a disc: it looks round when it lies on its flat surface. In a hereditary blood disease of man, the red cells are reduced in number and exhibit the form of a sickle, hence the name of the disease: sickle-cell anemia. The sickle hemoglobin is different from the normal hemoglobin in a number of properties (Table I).

But the differences have been traced back to one amino acid. By mild digestion, the hemoglobin can be cut into small peptides. As discovered by Vernon Ingram, one of these peptides is different in the normal and mutated proteins. In the sickle hemoglobin S, the

Table I. Amino Acids Sequence in Normal and Abnormal Hemoglobins.

Peptide fragments of normal hemoglobin (A), sickle-cell hemoglobin (S), and hemoglobin (C), associated with the so-called "hemoglobin C disease."

A	S	C
Histidine	Histidine	Histidine
Valine	Valine	Valine
Leucine	Leucine	Leucine
Leucine	Leucine	Leucine
Threonine	Threonine	Threonine
Proline	Proline	Proline
Glutamic acid	*Valine*	*Lysine*
Glutamic acid	Glutamic acid	Glutamic acid
Lysine	Lysine	Lysine

glutamic acid is replaced by valine. In hemoglobin C, glutamic acid is replaced by lysine.

Thus we have learned that nucleic acid is the substrate of hereditary properties, and that the genes control the synthesis of specific proteins, or of specific enzymes. We know that the sequence of nucleic bases in the genetic material is responsible for the sequence of amino acids in the proteins. We know that the replacement of one base pair by another may be responsible for a mutation. We also know that the difference between the normal and the mutated protein may be due to the replacement of one amino acid by another. As a consequence of the replacement of one base pair by another in the gene, one amino acid is replaced by another in the protein. The sequence is changed, and as a consequence the folding of the polypeptide chain might be changed too. The nucleic acid, the genetic material, is the substrate of the structural, hereditary change. The protein is the agent through which the hereditary change is expressed.

Reproduction of the Genetic Material

DNA. The genetic material, or the genetic information, is, *by definition*, transmitted from the mother cell to the daughter cell, that is, multiplied. How does one molecule of nucleic acid produce two identical molecules? How has nucleic acid solved the problem of molecular reproduction? Desoxyribonucleic acid is a double helix in which adenine and thymine on the one hand and guanine and cytosine on the other hand are united face to face by hydrogen bonds. The double helix is thus composed of two complementary strands. Watson and Crick in 1953 put forward the hypothesis that each strand acts as a template for the organization of a complementary one.

As the two strands of the duplex are complementary, the separation of the two strands cannot be described as a binary fission; it is, in fact, an inequational cleavage, the separation of two different parts. But as these parts are complementary, each one, when producing its complement, reproduces the original molecule. The unit, which is the molecule, is made up of two firmly bound complementary parts. The molecule of DNA cannot grow and does not grow. But by making use of complementarity it has solved the problem of molecular reproduction.

By the template mechanism, a single strand of nucleic acid can produce a molecule of protein. It can also produce a complementary nucleic strand, which in turn can reproduce the original one. But only a molecule made of two complementary structures can reproduce directly its own structure.

This is all right on paper, but how are things in the living system? An enzyme has been isolated from a bacterium that polymerizes desoxyribonucleotides. If these building blocks of DNA are added in a test tube together with the enzyme, DNA is synthesized. The necessary condition, however, is the presence of a DNA primer. The original DNA, the primer, may be multiplied *in vitro* by a factor of 10.

In DNA, as already mentioned, adenine is bound to thymine, guanine to cytosine. The ratio adenine/thymine, like the ratio guanine/cytosine, is equal to 1. But, in bacteria, the ratio (adenine + thymine)/(guanine + cytosine) varies from 0.6 to 2.8 according to the species.

What happens when these various types of DNA are taken as primers?

First: The ratio adenine/thymine and guanine/cytosine is always 1.

Second: The synthesis does not take place if one of the bases is missing.

Third: Each base can be replaced by an analogue, provided its hydrogen-bonding capacities are in agreement with the Watson-Crick model.

Fourth: The ratio $(A + T)/(G + C)$ in the synthesized DNA is the same as in the primer. If the "nonnatural" synthetic primer does not contain guanine or cytosine, these bases are absent in the newly formed DNA, despite being present in the test tube.

Fifth: When the DNA primer is heated, the two strands separate, and the rate of synthesis is markedly increased.

Everything happens as if one of the strands would act as a

template. Experimental data obtained so far are in full agreement with the Watson-Crick hypothesis.

Can we learn something more? Three mechanisms could be envisaged for the replication of the DNA. These are called conservative, semiconservative, and dispersive (Figure 10).

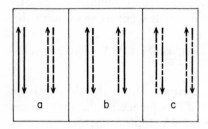

Figure 10.

(*a*) Conservative Mechanism.
   The duplex is reproduced as a whole.
(*b*) Semiconservative Mechanism.
   Each chain serves as a template for the production of a complementary one.
(*c*) Dispersive Mechanism.
   Pieces of the parental chains are scattered among the offspring duplexes.

a. In the *conservative* mechanism, the duplex is reproduced as a whole: one of the daughter duplexes is the parent, the other one entirely new.

b. In the *semiconservative* mechanism, each chain serves as template for the production of another complementary one. In this model, each of the daughter duplexes is composed of two parts: one chain is parental, the other new. This is the original hypothesis put forward by Crick and Watson in 1953.

c. In the *dispersive* mechanism, the integrity of the chains is not maintained. Pieces of the parental chains are scattered among the daughter duplexes.

In order to answer our question, an experiment is needed. It consists of labeling the DNA of the parent organism and following the distribution of the label in the offspring. The first experiment of this kind was done by Cyrus Levinthal in 1956. Bacteriophage was selected as the material. Its DNA was labeled with radioactive phosphorus, and the concentration of hot phosphorus was measured in the daughter bacteriophage. The conclusion was that DNA reproduces by the semiconservative mechanism, that is, in agreement with the original Watson-Crick hypotheses. A number of experiments performed since on various materials seem to agree with this conclusion.

PRODUCTION OF AN RNA TEMPLATE FROM DNA. Three mechanisms have been considered.

1. The single-stranded RNA is formed within the deep groove of the DNA double helix. The specific sequence of the RNA bases is governed by the base pairs of the DNA duplex. Each of the bases of the base pair of the duplex could, according to Stent, form another pair of hydrogen bonds with a third base. If the bond between the C of the sugar and the N of the base is to be always in the same position, a given pair of the duplex bases would combine with only one base of the future RNA.

2. Each of the two strands of the DNA duplex forms an RNA chain. As the two chains of the double DNA helix are complementary, the two RNA chains would be different. One could of course be active, the other inactive.

3. Only one of the strands of the DNA duplex produces an RNA chain, the other being inactive.

The problem of the mechanism by which the DNA produces the RNA template for the synthesis of proteins, and more generally an RNA molecule, is not yet solved.

REPRODUCTION OF RNA. The same type of problem is posed by RNA, which is the genetic material of a number of animal viruses and of plant viruses. Here again, an enzyme has been discovered which binds ribonucleotides and organizes them in long chains. RNA is single-stranded. The formation of a complementary strand by the template mechanism would end in two chains with qualitatively different genetic information. But it could well be that only one — let us say A — possesses the right sequence of triplets suitable for the coding of amino acids and the synthesis of proteins. The other — let us say B — would be able to produce only a complementary RNA strand A. It could also be that a temporary RNA double helix is formed, or that the single-stranded RNA produces a double-stranded DNA. The mechanism would be the reverse of the synthesis of RNA from DNA. Anyhow, the problem is not solved — not yet solved. Let us, for the time being, forget the question of the replication of the ribonucleic acid and of viruses containing ribonucleic acid.

Conclusions

The conclusion has been reached that each organism contains a structure, desoxyribonucleic acid, which is the very base of hereditary order. This structure contains the information for the production of specific templates and of specific proteins. Because DNA is composed of two complementary strands, its reproduction is the production by each of the strands of a complementary one. The specificity of nucleic acid is the sequence of the nucleic bases, and the specificity of proteins is the sequence of the amino acids. A change in the base sequence results in a change in the nucleic acid specificity.

"If it be true," wrote Max Delbrück in 1949, "that the essence of life is the accumulation of experience through the generations, then, one may perhaps suspect that the key problem of biology, from the physicist's point of view, is how living matter manages to record and perpetuate experience." The key problem is now solved.

REFERENCES

Anfinsen, C. B. (1959). *The Molecular Basis of Evolution.* John Wiley & Sons, New York.
Baldwin, E. (1947). *Dynamic Aspects of Biochemistry.* The University Press, Cambridge.
Dunn, L. C., ed. (1951). *Genetics in the 20th Century.* The Macmillan Company, New York.

Fruton, J. S., and Simmonds, S. (1953). *General Biochemistry*. John Wiley & Sons, New York.

Levinthal, C. (1956). The mechanism of DNA replication and genetic recombination in phage. *Proc. Nat. Acad. Sci.*, *42*, 394–404.

McElroy, W. D., and Glass, B., eds. (1957). *A Symposium on the Chemical Basis of Heredity*. The Johns Hopkins Press, Baltimore.

Rich, A. (1959). Polynucleotide interactions and the nucleic acids. *Brookhaven Symposia in Biology*, *12*, 17–26.

Wagner, R. P., and Mitchell, H. K. (1955). *Genetics and Metabolism*. John Wiley & Sons, New York.

IV. THE FUNCTIONAL ORDER

The Problem

Life has been equated with a complex hereditary order involving a specific sequence of nucleic bases. The fiber of nucleic acid, the genetic material, contains the information for the synthesis of enzymes. Each enzyme is a specific sequence of amino acids which performs only one chemical reaction. Growth and multiplication depend on the completion of two sets of processes (Figure 11). In the first phase, the building blocks — the nucleic bases and the amino acids — are synthesized step by step. In the second phase, the building blocks are assembled in an orderly way into specific proteins and specific nucleic acids. For the first process, only enzymes are required. The second process involves specific templates, DNA or RNA. Thus more enzymes and more nucleic acids are produced. This is growth. When the genetic material has duplicated, the double mother divides into two daughter cells. This is reproduction.

A bacterium contains about 2,000 genes and 2,000 enzymes. In a factory involving the activity of a few thousand workers, somebody, or something, has to co-ordinate and to orient the activity of the individual units, which, as parts of a whole, are interdependent subunits. If the factory manufactures cars, a given balance must exist between the number of motors, wheels, doors, brakes, etc. Moreover, the rate of production has to be adjusted to the consumption of cars; that is, it depends on extrinsic factors. The units of the factory, the workers, are parts of a whole; that is, they are interdependent units. In a factory, different types of devices controlling order are interacting at various levels.

The cell is a factory. It has to synthesize all the building blocks in the right proportions and in the right amounts. A substance produced in excess means waste. And waste decreases the chances in

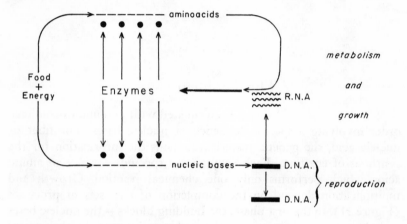

Figure 11. Metabolism, Growth, and Reproduction.

Food is metabolized. The small building blocks, the essential metabolites (amino acids and nucleic bases), are synthesized. Nucleic bases are organized into nucleic acids. The duplication of the desoxyribonucleic acid (DNA) is the very basis of reproduction. The manufacture of ribonucleic acid is the prerequisite for protein synthesis. Amino acids will be patternized into specific protein on the ribonucleic acid templates.

the struggle for life. A balance also has to be maintained between the various macromolecules, especially between nucleic acids and proteins. An imbalance may lead to cellular disease and even to death. Moreover, organisms do not live in a constant environment. This is true especially for bacteria. In nature, they encounter a wide variety of conditions. And in the laboratory, these poor beasts are submitted to terrifying ill-treatment.

The statement that the organism reproduces true to type is

statistically correct. But what is reproduced true to type is the genetic material. The enzymatic equipment of a bacterium is far from being constant. It varies quantitatively as well as qualitatively. The potentialities of the organism are under the control of the genetic material, but the functioning of the genetic material and of the whole organism is subject to the action of the environment. The organism has to cope with the environmental changes as well as to ensure the harmonious interplay of its enzymes. We have to disclose the mechanism by which the genetic material is informed of what happens in the cytoplasm and in the outer world. How are the orders transmitted from one macromolecule to the other? What is the basis of molecular interaction and balance? The cell, the integrated system of specific interdependent macromolecules, will be studied as a functional unit. As an introduction, two models will be considered: one of induction of enzyme synthesis, the other of inhibition of enzyme synthesis.

Two Models of Enzyme Synthesis

INDUCTION. Some strains of the bacterium *Escherichia coli* are able to utilize lactose as a carbon or energy source. Lactose is a disaccharide in which glucose and galactose are united by a β-galactosidic link. The enzyme that controls its metabolism splits the β-galactosidic bond and is therefore called β-galactosidase. As a result of its activity, lactose is hydrolyzed into glucose and galactose. This is a prerequisite for the utilization of lactose.

Bacteria grown in a synthetic medium where the only organic compound is lactose contain the enzyme galactosidase — about 6,000 molecules per bacterium. Bacteria grown in a medium containing glycerol are completely devoid of enzyme. If lactose is supplied, however, the synthesis of the galactosidase starts after a lag of a few minutes, and within an hour or so each bacterium has manufactured its full load of enzyme. Thus, galactosidase is synthesized only when lactose or a few other β-galactosides are present. Lactose induces the synthesis of galactosidase. In the absence of galactosidase, the bacteria are unable to grow in a medium containing lactose as the sole carbon and energy source. When no lactose is present, the enzyme is useless. The induced synthesis of the enzyme increases the fitness between the bacterium and its environment. It is why this process has been, for a long time, called enzymatic adaptation. It is now described as an induced biosynthesis of enzyme. Let us now consider the reverse process.

REPRESSION. The bacterium *Escherichia coli* is able to grow in a synthetic medium devoid of any amino acid. Such a bacterium is therefore able to synthesize all its building blocks, or essential metabolites, and, among them, the amino acid methionine. The last step in the synthesis of methionine is catalyzed by an enzyme called methionine synthase.

When growing in a synthetic medium, the bacteria contain methionine synthase. Of course they have to. For in the absence of methionine synthase, they are unable to synthesize methionine. And in the absence of methionine, they are unable to synthesize proteins, that is, to grow. The enzyme methionine synthase is actually present (Figure 12). What happens when the growth

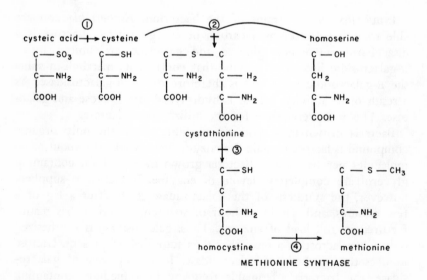

Figure 12. The Synthesis of the Amino Acid Methionine.

medium is supplemented with methionine? A labeled methionine is utilized, a methionine with a hot sulfur atom. The labeled methionine is taken up. And, after a few hours, the bacteria are assayed for methionine synthase: the enzyme has disappeared. This means that in the presence of extrinsic methionine, the synthesis of the enzyme is blocked. This phenomenon, the inhibition of enzyme synthesis, is called repression.

Suppose now that the bacterium is growing in the absence of methionine, and that it produces an excess of methionine. This excess can be due either to an excess of enzyme or to a decreased rate of utilization of methionine. The result is the same, that is, an excess of methionine. But, as a result of this excess, the synthesis of the responsible enzyme is repressed, and as a consequence the synthesis of methionine decreases. A balanced state is reached which corresponds to an equal production and consumption of methionine.

Repression of enzyme synthesis thus increases the fitness between the bacterium and its environment. Whether we deal with the utilization of the carbon and energy source, namely the sugar lactose, or with the synthesis of an essential building block, namely the amino acid methionine, we observe an adjustment of the enzymatic system. The cell tends toward a physiological balance. Our problem is to learn what the responsible mechanism is.

The development of genetics and the chemical identification of the genetic material have been possible because of the existence of hereditary variation called mutations. The development of our knowledge concerning the functional order has been possible, thanks to the existence of nonhereditary, not transmissible variation, such as the induced synthesis of enzymes or the repression of enzyme synthesis. Let us consider next the problem of the interactions of genes and of enzymes.

The Genetic Control
of Bacterial Metabolism

METABOLISM OF LACTOSE. *Escherichia coli* will be taken as a tool. The bacterium is surrounded by a cell wall whose function is mainly to counteract the internal osmotic pressure. The cytoplasm is limited by a thin membrane. Among the remarkable properties of the bacterium is selective permeability. A bacterium is not permeable to everything. And it was discovered that the penetration inside the bacterium of many small molecules is mediated by a given specific enzyme called permease. There is one specific permease for the amino acid tryptophan, another for the amino acid methionine, another for the sugar glucose, another one for lactose, etc. (Figure 13).

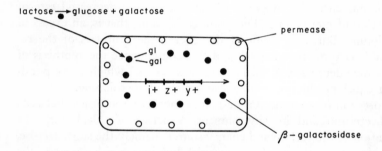

Figure 13. The Utilization of Lactose.

Schematic representation of a bacterium. The two structural genes y and z control the synthesis of the β-galactoside permease and the β-galactosidase, respectively.

The permease is responsible for the specific transfer of lactose and other β-galactosides across the membrane; the β-galactosidase splits lactose into glucose and galactose. The gene i controls inductivity versus constitutivity.

Thus, the metabolism of lactose is controlled by a specific permease. Its role is just to take the molecules of lactose in the environment and to transfer them across the membrane, a reaction in which an acetylation is perhaps involved. Once lactose has been pumped into the cytoplasm, it is split into glucose and galactose by the enzyme β-galactosidase. Our original model bacterium possesses both permease and β-galactosidase. Both enzymes are synthesized only when lactose is present. Lactose is an inducer. Accordingly, the enzymes are said to be inductive. *Inductive* means here, as in logic, "based upon or using induction."

VARIATIONS. This original model can give rise to hereditary variants, to mutants belonging to various categories:

(*a*) The bacteria able to synthesize β-galactosidase may give rise to variants unable to perform the synthesis; z^+ being the symbol for the character carrying the information for the galactosidase, the mutation is $z^+ \rightleftharpoons z^-$.

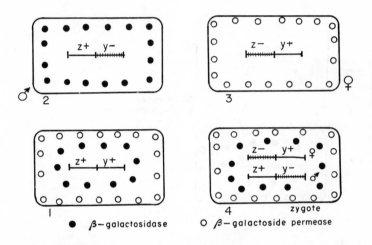

Figure 14. Genes z and y as Independent Units.

The z and y genes control the synthesis of β-galactosidase and β-galactoside permease, respectively.
1. The bacterium is z^+ and y^+: both enzymes are manufactured.
2. The bacterium is z^+ and y^-: only β-galactosidase is produced.
3. The bacterium is z^- and y^+: only permease is formed.
4. The zygote resulting from the injection of the male chromosome $z^+ \ y^-$ in the $z^- \ y^+$ female manufactures both enzymes, despite the fact that the genes z^+ and y^+ are located on different chromosomes (position *trans*).

(*b*) The bacteria able to perform the synthesis of permease may give rise to mutants unable to perform the synthesis of permease; y^+ being the symbol for the character carrying the information for the synthesis of permease, the mutation is $y^+ \rightleftharpoons y^-$ (Figure 14).

(*c*) The inductive bacteria may give rise to mutants that produce β-galactosidase and permease in the absence of an inducer. They are called constitutive; i^+ being the symbol for the character controlling inductivity versus constitutivity, the mutation is $i^+ \leftrightarrows i^-$, where i^+ stands for inductivity, i^- for constitutivity (Figure 15).

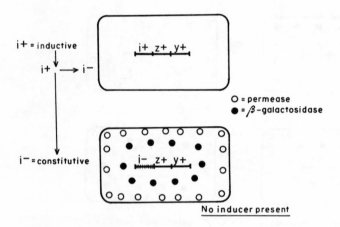

Figure 15. Mutation from Inductivity toward Constitutivity.

The bacterium carrying the gene i^+ is inductive: in the absence of inducer, it manufactures neither permease nor β-galactosidase, despite the presence of both genes z^+ and y^+. If the gene i^+ mutates toward constitutivity (i^-), both enzymes are synthesized in the absence of an inducer.

These variations are hereditary. And as the substrate of heredity in bacteria is the nucleic acid of the chromosome, it seems probable that the three features, or characters — inductivity, synthesis of β-galactosidase, synthesis of permease — are each controlled by a unit of genetic material, by a specific gene. That the substrate of hereditary information is really located in the chromosome and is a unit of function is easy to show, with the help of recombination. A digression is necessary here.

THE GENE AS A UNIT; SEXUAL DIGRESSION. Our bacterium exhibits sexual processes. When males are mixed with females, they conjugate. The chromosome of the male is injected slowly into the female, the process lasting around one hour. If the couples are put in a Waring Blendor, the friction forces separate the partners, and conjugation is interrupted. If this is done at intervals, one finds that each gene of the male enters the female at a given fixed time, and that the various genes always enter in the same order. This allows us to locate the place of each gene on the chromosome. This order can be verified by the classical tests of genetics, namely, the determination of the frequency of exchange of one piece of a chromosome for another. This gives a measure of the relative distance of the genes.

When these types of experiments are performed, one finds:

1. that the characters of the male can be transferred to the female.
2. that the three "genes," z, y, and i, controlling the utilization of lactose, are closely associated or linked.

As already seen, the different genes, i^+, z^+, y^+, can mutate independently, and all possible types of combination are found. Are these genes parts of the same functional unit, or do they represent different functional units? How can we know that the units are different? What justifies the use of the term "unit"?

ALTERED ENZYMES. It is supposed that a gene, or its corresponding template, produces a protein, as a whole, by a sort of zipper-like mechanism. Let us now consider the gene z (Figure 16). The

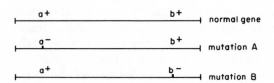

Figure 16. Gene Mutation.

The normal gene possesses the structure a^+ b^+. A point mutation, a replacement of one base pair by another, can take place on various sectors of the gene, for example in a ($a^+ \longrightarrow a^-$) or in b ($b^+ \longrightarrow b^-$).

structure a^+b^+ corresponds to the "normal" gene z^+, that is, to the information for the synthesis of the enzyme. A gene is a sequence of nucleic bases, and any nucleic base, whether in position a or b, can be replaced by another (Table II). As a result, one

Table II. The Activity of Normal and Mutated Genes.

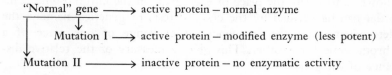

"Normal" gene ⟶ active protein – normal enzyme

Mutation I ⟶ active protein – modified enzyme (less potent)

Mutation II ⟶ inactive protein – no enzymatic activity

sequence of bases is replaced by another, and in the protein one amino acid is replaced by another. The normal gene z^+ produces the enzyme. The mutated gene z^- does not produce the original enzyme, but instead a new, altered protein. It may have a slight enzymatic activity, or be totally devoid of activity. An important fraction of the negative mutants z^- nevertheless contains a protein able to cross-react with the anti-β-galactosidase antibody and to displace β-galactosidase when combined with the antibody. Some z^- mutants give a complete cross-reaction; that is, they are able to displace entirely the enzyme from the enzyme-antibody complex. Some others give incomplete cross-reactions; that is, they can saturate only a fraction (20 to 60 per 100) of the antibody.

All this shows that the mutations affecting the gene z^+ are manifold. The proteins produced by the various z^- mutants differ from the enzyme β-galactosidase and differ also in each of the mutants. So when the gene $z^+(a^+b^+)$, the normal structure, is present, the enzyme is synthesized (Figure 17). When the mutated gene z^-, whether a^- or b^-, is present, no enzyme is synthesized. Now the mutants a^- and b^- are different. Let us then mix the various z^- mutants. The male carries a gene a^+b^- and the female a gene a^-b^+. The zygote has two different sets of genes and is therefore called heterozygote for gene z. Such a heterozygote is unable to manufacture β-galactosidase, despite the presence of all the information. In

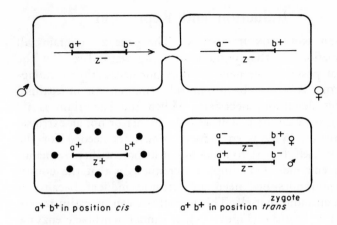

$a^+ b^+$ in position *cis* $a^+ b^+$ in position *trans*

Figure 17. The Gene z as a Unit.

When the gene is z^+ ($a^+ b^+$), β-galactosidase is synthesized (lower-left corner) and $a^+ b^+$ are located on the same chromosome (position *cis*).

The mutated gene $a^+ b^-$ (male) or $a^- b^+$ (female) is unable to "produce" the enzyme. The heterozygote (lower-right corner) does not manufacture the enzyme: a^+ and b^+ are located on a different chromosome (position *trans*), and there is no complementary relation.

this case, the information carried on two *separate* genes — that is, in position *trans* — is useless. The structure z can function only as a unit. In the modern terminology, z is a *cistron*. The locus z thus contains the genetic information for the molecule of β-galactosidase. A number of experiments have provided good evidence that it contains all of this information. The gene z functions as a whole. In order that a protein be synthesized, all of the information has to be present in one and the same structure (position *cis*). There is no complementary relation between two different mutants of the same gene. The gene, or better the *cistron*, is therefore a unit of information and of function.

By the same technique, it is possible to show that the synthesis of the permease is controlled by a unit y, different from the unit z. Finally, inductivity is itself controlled by another unit, i, different from y and z.

Induction and Repression

GENERALIZED INDUCTION HYPOTHESIS. The gene z^+ contains all of the information for the synthesis of a β-galactosidase. But the bacterium that possesses the gene z^+ does not necessarily manufacture the enzyme. When the bacterium is i^+ (inductive), an extrinsic inducer is, by definition, necessary. When the bacterium is i^- (constitutive), the enzyme is synthesized whether or not an extrinsic inducer is present. Why is an inducer sometimes needed for the gene to express itself, that is, to make use of its potentiality by manufacturing the enzyme? The simplest hypothesis is that the constitutive bacterium does not need an extrinsic inducer because it manufactures an inducer itself. This hypothesis can be easily tested.

One takes a z^-i^- male (Figure 18). It cannot synthesize enzyme because it does not possess the right information. But it possesses the constitutive gene i^-. It could produce enzyme in the absence of an inducer if it were z^+.

One takes a z^+i^+ female that possesses the right information for the synthesis of the enzyme; but, being i^+ (inductive), it is unable to manufacture enzyme in the absence of an inducer. Now males and females are mixed. The male injects its chromosome into the female. If the theory is right, if the function of the gene i^- is to manufacture an inducer, then the zygote should synthesize the enzyme in the absence of an extrinsic inducer. It does not. Things are more complicated than was thought. Another hypothesis has to be considered: the gene i^+ manufactures a repressor.

THE REPRESSOR. The reverse experiment is then performed. The male is z^+i^+ instead of the female, and the female is z^-i^- instead of the male. In the absence of an inducer, the male cannot manufacture the enzyme because it is inductive. And the constitutive female cannot manufacture the enzyme because it is z^-. Male and female are again mixed in the absence of an inducer. As soon as the z^+i^+ gene from the male has penetrated in the z^-i^- female, the heterozygote z^+i^+/z^-i^- starts producing β-galactosidase at full speed.

Let us then admit that the gene i^+ does synthesize a repressor, the gene i^- being unable to do so. In the zygote type I, the female cytoplasm corresponds to the gene i^+, that is, to inductivity. A

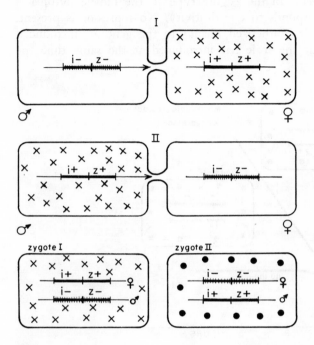

Figure 18. The Repressor.

I. The constitutive male i⁻ does not manufacture enzyme in the absence of an inducer because it is z⁻. The inductive female i⁺ does not manufacture enzyme in the absence of inducer, despite the presence of z⁺, because a repressor is present (repressor is represented by crosses). The corresponding zygote (zygote I) does not produce enzyme in the absence of an inducer, despite the presence of the constitutive gene i⁻, because the cytoplasm of the inductive female contains a repressor. The gene i⁺ is dominant.

II. The inductive male does not manufacture enzyme in the absence of an inducer because a repressor is present. The constitutive female does not manufacture the enzyme because it is z⁻. The corresponding zygote (zygote II) will produce enzyme for a limited time (see next part of figure), because the z⁺ gene coming from the male has entered into a constitutive cytoplasm (devoid of repressor).

The two zygotes (I and II) have the same genetic constitution, but zygote I has an inductive cytoplasm (the female is i⁺), whereas zygote II has a constitutive one (the female is i⁻).

repressor is present. In the zygote type II, the female cytoplasm is i⁻. This corresponds to constitutivity. No repressor is present, and the enzyme is synthesized, thanks to the gene z⁺ introduced by the male. But the male has introduced at the same time the

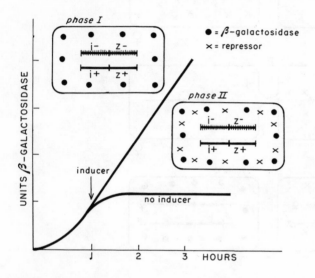

Figure 19. Synthesis of β-Galactosidase by a Heterozygote.

The heterozygote of type II shown in the preceding figure has been formed by the transfer of the male genes i⁺ z⁺ into the i⁻ z⁻ female. The female, being constitutive (i⁻), is devoid of repressor, and β-galactosidase is synthesized, in the absence of an inducer, as soon as the gene z⁺ enters the female. This is the first phase. But the male has introduced also the inductive gene i⁺: a repressor is synthesized, and the synthesis of galactosidase stopped. This is the second phase. If, however, an inducer is added, the synthesis of the enzyme continues.

gene i⁺, which, according to the hypothesis, should be responsible for the manufacture of a repressor. Something seems to be wrong. If, however, the synthesis of galactosidase is followed long enough, it is then found that the rate of enzyme synthesis decreases and reaches a zero value (Figure 19). A repressor has really been formed.

If an inducer is added after the synthesis has stopped, the production of enzyme starts anew.

The genetic analysis has thus revealed a number of important facts. The genes z, y, and i are independent units of function and therefore are different genes. Thus, the small sector of the bacterial chromosome that controls the synthesis of the enzymes responsible for the metabolism of lactose, and more generally of β-galactosides, is composed of three units. Two of them, z and y, carry the information for the synthesis, respectively, of galactosidase and permease. They are called *structural genes*. The other, i, determines the constitutive as opposed to the inductive type of synthesis of both enzymes. It is called a *regulating gene*. Things happen as if the gene i^+ controlling the inductive state corresponded to the synthesis of a repressor, the mutation $i^+ \rightarrow i^-$ to the loss of the ability to form a repressor, hence to a constitutive situation. The repressor has not yet been identified. But a number of data are in favor of the hypothesis that it is a ribonucleic acid.

The Ways of Repression

REPRESSOR, APOREPRESSOR, COREPRESSOR, AND INDUCER; THE CONTROL OF ENZYME SYNTHESES. For the bacterium, lactose is a carbon source and a source of energy. It is part of the food. The bacterium may be fed with other organic compounds, such as glycerol or pyruvic acid. The food that a bacterium may find depends on the hazards of its daily life. The bacterium obviously cannot afford to manufacture a large number of useless enzymes. And it is quite natural that the synthesis of the contingent enzymes is regulated. Let us consider the enzymes responsible for the synthesis of the essential building blocks and especially of amino acids.

AMINO ACIDS. It has already been stated that if the amino acid methionine is provided, the bacterium stops synthesizing methionine synthase, the enzyme responsible for the last step in the biosynthesis of methionine. The product of enzymatic activity stops the synthesis of the enzyme. This mechanism is known to be quite general, and a few cases have been studied extensively. One, for example, is the biosynthesis of the amino acid arginine. In a medium devoid of arginine, the bacterium synthesizes arginine. If arginine is supplied, the enzymes cease to be produced. The end product of the chain of biosynthesis blocks the synthesis of all the enzymes involved in the chain of arginine biosynthesis. Thus, if an excess of arginine is produced, the synthesis of the enzymes involved in its synthesis is specifically repressed, and less arginine will be produced. The same mechanism is operative in a number of biosynthetic pathways, such as nucleic bases, histidine and tryptophan. Only the case of tryptophan will be discussed here.

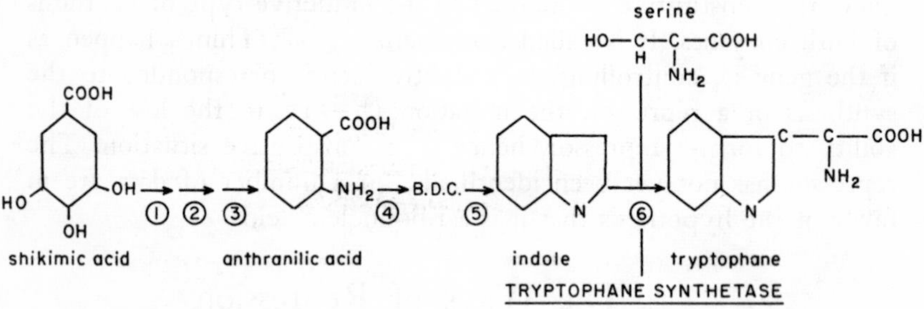

Figure 20. The Biosynthesis of the Amino Acid Tryptophan.

In a synthetic medium devoid of tryptophan, tryptophan is synthesized by a system of enzymes (Figure 20). If tryptophan is added, the synthesis of the enzymes is stopped, that is, repressed. Let us admit that the synthesis is blocked by a repressor. This repressor is specific; it is known to act only on the tryptophan enzymes and not on the synthesis of any other system, as shown in Table III. From the original repressed bacterium, it is possible to isolate mutants that are called *derepressed*. In these mutants, the synthesis of the tryptophan enzymes is not blocked any more by tryptophan. The bacteria produce much more tryptophan than needed, and this excess tryptophan is excreted. If tryptophan is added to the medium, the synthesis of the enzymes responsible for the synthesis of tryptophan is not altered in the derepressed strain, whereas it is inhibited

Table III. Action of Tryptophan on Enzyme Synthesis.

	Shikimic acid $\xrightarrow{1}$ $\xrightarrow{2}$ $\xrightarrow{3}$	anthranilic acid	$\xrightarrow{4}$ $\xrightarrow{5}$	C.D.B.	$\xrightarrow{6}$	indole	$\xrightarrow{7}$	tryptophan
R⁺$_{try}$ (repressed)	R		R$^{(°)}$				R	
R⁻$_{try}$ (derepressed)	O		O				O	

(°) Even if enzyme 6 missing, R, repressed; O, not repressed.
C.D.B. Blue diazotized compound.
Tryptophan represses the synthesis of enzymes in the normal repressed R⁺$_{try}$ strain but not in the derepressed R⁻$_{try}$ mutant.

in the normal strain. Let us admit that the original wild type possesses the gene R^+_{try}, which is able to manufacture the repressor, and that the derepressed bacterium carries a mutated gene R^-_{try}, unable to manufacture the repressor. R^+ and R^- bacteria are allowed to conjugate. A zygote is thus formed, carrying both R^+_{try} and R^-_{try} genes. In this heterozygote, the synthesis of the tryptophan enzyme is blocked. A repressor is obviously produced by the R^+ gene, which is dominant over the R^- gene (Table IV).

Table IV. Enzyme Synthesis as Affected by Tryptophan in a Repressed and a Derepressed Bacterium and in the Heterozygote.

> The derepressed bacteria contain three to seven times more enzymes than the repressed one. The addition of tryptophan is without effect on the enzyme level in the derepressed strain, whereas it blocks enzyme synthesis in the repressed one. The heterozygote behaves like the repressed strain: the character "repressed" is dominant.

	Level of tryptophan synthetase		
	R^+_{try} repressed	R^-_{try} derepressed	R^+/R^- heterozygote repressed
Without tryptophan	100	300–700	100
Tryptophan added	8	300–700	8

The study of the tryptophan repression leads to an important conclusion. In the derepressed bacterium, tryptophan is produced in excess; nevertheless, there is no inhibition of enzyme synthesis. This means that in the normal strain, it is not tryptophan itself which is the repressor, but something produced with the help of tryptophan.

The hypothesis has been proposed that the regulating gene R^+ produces an inactive aporepressor. Tryptophan is the corepressor that combines with the aporepressor to form the repressor proper.

Whether the tryptophan has been manufactured by the bacterium or pumped from the medium into the bacterium, the result is the same.

CARBON AND ENERGY SOURCE. How does the aporepressor-repressor hypothesis apply to the regulation of enzymes involved in the metabolism of the carbon and energy source?

When lactose is present as the sole carbon and energy source, the bacterium "needs" galactosidase in order to grow, and it starts synthesizing it, provided it possesses the corresponding genetic information.

How does lactose induce the synthesis of the enzyme? It is perhaps simpler to consider first the inhibition of the synthesis. When bacteria are growing in a medium containing glucose *and* lactose, no β-galactosidase is produced by the z^+ bacteria. Glucose is used up first, and the synthesis of β-galactosidase starts, but only after a negative phase that lasts around 30 minutes. Things happen as if in the presence of glucose a repressor has been produced. The theory is that a product of the metabolism of glucose acts as a corepressor which combines with an aporepressor. As long as this repressor is present, no β-galactosidase is synthesized. When it has disappeared as a result of the cellular metabolism, the synthesis of the enzyme can start.

Why then is lactose necessary? Glucose has been used up in the first phase of the bacterial development. But when it is used up, metabolism continues at the expense of the reserves that the bacterium has stocked. A corepressor perhaps continues to be produced, but it has less affinity for the aporepressor than the product of glucose metabolism. Lactose competes for the aporepressor with this hypothetical corepressor of low affinity and thus prevents the formation of the repressor. The β-galactosidase is synthesized and functions: lactose is hydrolyzed into glucose and galactose. The latter are used up in the metabolic processes. If glucose is used up entirely, a corepressor is not produced or is not available. But if an excess of β-galactosidase is synthesized, an excess of glucose is produced as a result of its activity. A corepressor will be formed and, consequently, a repressor. The synthesis of the enzyme responsible for the metabolism of lactose will be repressed. In view of the relatively rapid adjustment of enzyme synthesis to the need, this hypothesis implies that the repressor is unstable and that its half-life is short, let us say a few minutes.

The question will immediately be asked: How does β-galactosidase behave in a constitutive bacterium? Some bacteria are constitutive because they do not produce a repressor, some others because the "operator" (explained in the next section) is insensitive to the repressor. In both cases, whether or not lactose is present, the bacterium contains β-galactosidase. Estimates show that the constitutive bacteria contain about 30% more enzyme than the inductive ones. Enzyme synthesis is of course limited by something, let us say by the availability of amino acids. Anyhow, in a medium devoid of lactose, the enzyme is useless.

When adaptive and constitutive bacteria are inoculated together into a medium devoid of lactose, the constitutive bacteria are outgrown by the adaptive ones and disappear, owing to natural selection. The growth rate of the constitutive bacteria is obviously lower than the growth rate of the adaptive ones. This is obviously due to the fact that part of the building blocks is utilized for the manufacture of a useless enzyme.

Evolution has thus ended in a remarkable device. When lactose is absent, no enzyme for its utilization is produced. When lactose is present, the enzyme is synthesized and the synthesis adjusted to the need.

Before any further discussion, a preliminary attempt at a generalization seems to be necessary. It might be stated that the synthesis of the enzymes required for the metabolism of the energy source is controlled by the over-all available energy sources. Moreover, the synthesis of the enzymes necessary for the synthesis of any given essential metabolites is controlled by the "level" of this essential metabolite. "Level" here means intracellular concentration, whether the essential metabolite is extrinsic or endogenous. The effector of the regulatory mechanism is a repressor. How does the repressor act?

THE OPERATOR. The structural gene carrying the information for the synthesis of a given enzyme will not express itself if a repressor is present. How does the repressor repress? Inductivity and constitutivity have to be considered anew.

In the cases studied so far, inductivity is "dominant." This conclusion is based on the consideration of a heterozygote containing two sets of chromosomes, one i^+z^+, the other i^-z^+. In the absence of an inducer, no enzyme, no β-galactosidase, is produced, despite the presence of the gene i^- responsible for constitutivity. The hypothesis is that the gene i^+ produces a repressor, and the expression of the structural gene z^+ of the chromosome i^-z^+ is blocked, despite the presence of the constitutive gene i^-. Thus, no enzyme is formed in the absence of an inducer. The gene i^+ imposes the inductive situation. The inductive gene i^+ is said to be dominant, and the constitutive gene i^-, recessive (Figure 21). The repressor produced thanks to the gene i^+ acts on the "constitutive" chromosome carrying the constitutive gene i^- or on the enzyme-forming system produced by the "constitutive" chromosome.

The problem of the site of action of the repressor was solved by the discovery of a new category of mutants. An extensive study has revealed that in some mutants constitutivity, instead of being recessive, is dominant. When constitutivity is dominant, the heterozygotes i^+z^+, i^-z^+ manufacture the β-galactosidase in the absence of inducer, despite the presence of the inductive gene i^+. An elaborate series of experiments has led to the conclusion that when a bacterium mutates from recessive to dominant constitutivity, a specific gene is involved which has been called the operator and designated by the letter o.

The dominant inductive would have the constitution $i^+o^+z^+$, the o^+ gene being "sensitive" to the repressor. The dominant constitutive would be $i^-o^cz^+$, the o^c gene being "insensitive" to the repressor. It was found that the mutation $o^+ \rightarrow o^c$ affects not only the gene z (for the β-galactosidase) but also the gene y (for the permease). But it affects only those genes located on the same chromosome, that is, in position *cis* (Figure 22).

Thanks to recombination experiments, it is known that the genes y and z are adjacent. Close to them is the operator gene o, and next to it the regulating gene i. The structural gene contains the information for the synthesis of the specific enzymes. The regulating gene produces — or does not produce — a specific repressor. The functional unit formed by the operator gene and the structural gene has been called an "operon."

The repressor formed by the combination of the aporepressor and

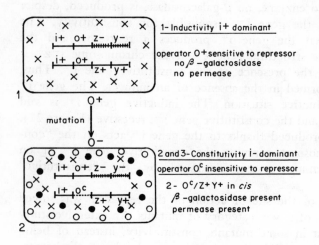

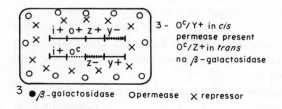

Figure 21. The Operator Gene.

1. Inductivity is dominant. The operator is of the wild type (o+) that is sensitive to the repressor. No enzymes are produced by the heterozygote in the absence of an inducer.

2. Constitutivity is dominant. The genes z+ and y+, located on the same chromosome as the constitutive operator oᶜ, are active: both permease and β-galactosidase are produced in the absence of an inducer, despite the presence of a repressor.

3. Constitutivity is dominant but only for the gene y+ located on the same chromosome as oᶜ (position *cis*). The gene z+ is located on a chromosome carrying the wild-type operator o+ and is not active.

of the corepressor would act on the operator gene. When the inductive bacterium i+ is o+, the operator is sensitive to the repressor. When the repressor is present, the operator gene is in position *stop*, and the two structural genes z+ and y+ are "blocked" and do not

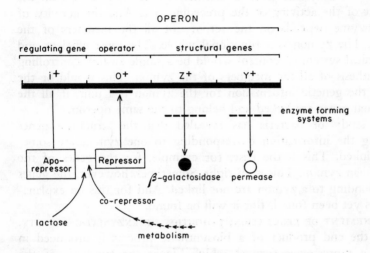

Figure 22. The Operon.

The structural genes z+ and y+ "manufacture," respectively, β-galactosidase and β-galactoside permease only in the absence of the repressor. The repressor is produced from an aporepressor synthesized by the gene i+ and a corepressor that is a product of metabolism of the energy source – glucose, for example. Lactose, the inducer, competes with the corepressor and prevents the formation of the repressor. When no repressor is present, the operator gene o+ is in position *go*, and the structural genes are active. When a repressor is present, the operator gene is in position *stop*, and enzyme synthesis is repressed.

produce the enzyme-forming system. When the repressor is absent, the operator gene is in position *go*. There is a new problem now, and the question must be asked: How does the operator gene act? We have every reason to believe that the operator does not send messages to the cytoplasm. One hypothesis is that it acts by inducing a functional change in the structural genes, but nothing more is known at the present time.

Co-ordinated control. The group of enzymes that is responsible for the synthesis of a given essential metabolite or more generally for a given sequence of reactions will be called a *zymon*. All the members of a zymon work in harmony. One enzyme acts on the product of the activity of the preceding one. And the activity of each enzyme depends on the activity of all the members of the zymon. The zymon is a functional whole. The most efficient and economical system of control would be a single system controlling the synthesis of all the members of the zymon. This would be the case if the genetic information for the zymon is a unit, if all the individual genes are linked and belong to the same operon.

The study of bacteria has revealed that the structural genes carrying the information corresponding to one zymon are sometimes linked. This is the case, for example, for the genes of the tryptophan zymon. This is all right. Sometimes, however, the genes corresponding to a zymon are not linked. And for this no explanation has yet been found. But it will be found.

Refinement of regulation; inhibition of enzymatic activity. When the end product of a biosynthetic process is produced in excess, a repressor is formed which blocks the synthesis of the corresponding enzymes. But the enzymes are there, and if they continued to function, the accumulation of the end product would continue. It happens that this accumulation is prevented by a very simple device. The end product of enzymatic activity inhibits, or blocks, the functioning of the first enzyme of the biosynthetic pathway. The other enzymes involved in the particular chain of biosynthesis are consequently deprived of their substrate, and the activity of the zymon is reduced or blocked (Figure 23). This condition is known to exist in the arginine and the tryptophan zymons.

Thus a dual mechanism controls the production of amino acids, and more generally of essential metabolites. When the output exceeds the consumption, that is, the need, the synthesis of the responsible enzymes is repressed, and the activity of the already existing enzymes is depressed or stopped.

Preclusive and corrective feedback mechanisms. Let us consider first the synthesis of an essential metabolite: tryptophan. A

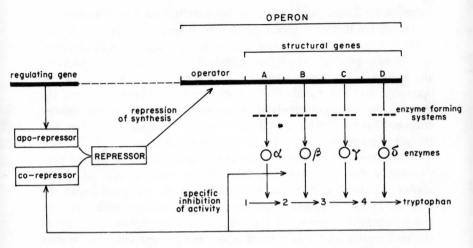

Figure 23. Control of the Activity and Synthesis of "Tryptophan Enzymes."

The activity of the systems of enzymes involved in the synthesis of tryptophan (tryptophan zymon) is under a dual control.

1. The activity of the first enzyme is specifically inhibited by tryptophan, the end product of the tryptophan zymon activity.

2. The synthesis of the tryptophan zymon is specifically inhibited by a repressor. The repressor is the result of the interaction of an aporepressor produced by a regulating gene and of tryptophan, which is a corepressor. The yet-hypothetical operator is in position *go* in the absence of repressor and is switched to *stop* by the repressor.

The term *zymon* is proposed to save time and money. Zymons belong to two categories: anazymons, which are responsible for anabolism, that is, syntheses; and catazymons, which deal with catabolism or breakdown. The system considered here is the tryptophan anazymon, whereas β-galactoside permease and β-galactosidase constitute the lactose catazymon.

bacterium synthesizes an excess of tryptophan, either because of a surplus of enzymes or because of a relative deficiency in the tryptophan consumption. The substance in excess, tryptophan, enters the constitution of a repressor. The operator, normally in position *go*, receives the signal *stop*. Tryptophan, the end product of a chain of enzymes, stops the synthesis of these enzymes. This is a true negative feedback mechanism: in this case the control is *corrective*.

Things are different when the energy source is concerned. When glucose is present, a repressor is produced, thanks to a corepressor that is a by-product of glucose metabolism. The repressor prevents the synthesis of β-galactosidase. The activity of the enzyme responsible for the metabolism of one energy source prevents the synthesis of a system involved in the metabolism of another energy source. This mechanism could be considered as a feedback, but it is in fact a *preventive*, or *preclusive*, counteraction.

The corrective feedback deals with the synthesis of an essential metabolite, the preclusive feedback with the metabolism of an energy source. In the first case, the corepressor is the end product of the activity of the enzymatic system submitted to repression, namely, the tryptophan zymon. In the other case, the repressor is one of the end products of a system of enzymes different from the system submitted to the repression. Obviously, many more systems have to be analyzed before any attempt at a generalization can be made.*

Conclusion

The study of enzyme synthesis has thus revealed that the cell is endowed with an elaborate dual mechanism which controls the activity and the synthesis of enzymes. The organism has to cope with the variation of the environment. In order to survive, it must adjust its enzymatic equipment according to the nature of its food and to the nature of its needs. And also, the machine must be regulated in such a way that each one of the four nucleic bases and each one of the twenty amino acids is manufactured in just the right amount and proportion.

The organism, the bacterium, has been compared to a factory. In a factory, one person, or one group of persons, directs the activity of all the others. Some readers may be tempted to ask the question: Who commands in a bacterium? Obviously, in a microorganism, no single molecule or group of molecules can be held responsible for

---

*The reader interested in the control of protein synthesis and in the problem of regulation is referred to the excellent review of Jacob and Monod, *J. Mol. Biol.* (1961), *3*, 318–356, to the last issue of the *Cold Spring Harbor Symposia on Quantitative Biology* (1961), *26*, and to Jacob and Wollman, *Sexuality and the Genetics of Bacteria*, Academic Press, New York, 1961.

the harmonious dynamic cellular balance. The functional order is the result of the interplay of the hereditary material, of the enzymes, of the metabolism, and of the dual feedback mechanism. The metabolism itself is the result of the interaction of enzymes and food, as provided by the environment.

In a computer, an essential part is the comparator. Its function is to compare the result of the work done by the machine with the information fed to the computer. When the work does not fit, it is simply suppressed. There is no such thing as a comparator in a microorganism. Instead, each organism takes part in a competition, the struggle for life, in which the functional values of the different types are compared. The comparison is a functional one. Evolution has necessarily selected the fittest types.

A specific function can only be the expression of a specific structure. The living organism has been defined as an independent unit of integrated structures and functions. This formula should now take on its full significance. Structures and functions are the complementary aspects of life. The organism is a functional system of order.

REFERENCES

Gaebler, O. H., ed. (1956). *Enzymes: Units of Biological Structure and Function* (Henry Ford Hospital, International Symposium). Academic Press, New York.

McElroy, W. D., and Glass, B., eds. (1958). *A Symposium on the Chemical Basis of Development*. The Johns Hopkins Press, Baltimore.

Monod, J. (1959). Biosynthese eines Enzyms. Information, Induktion, Repression. *Angew. Chemie, 71*, 685–691.

Wolstenholme, G. E. W., and O'Connor, C. M., eds. (1958). *Ciba Foundation Symposium on the Regulation of Cell Metabolism*. Little, Brown and Company, Boston.

V. VIRAL FUNCTIONS: ORDER AND DISORDER

Introduction

An organism is an orderly system of integrated structures and functions able to metabolize and to reproduce its kind. The microorganism or the cell is the ultimate unit of integration and reproduction. *Ultimate* here means smallest. The cell must have at its disposal some 2,000 enzyme species in order to secure energy and to synthesize all its building blocks. It must therefore possess the genetic information for the synthesis of these 2,000 enzymes and some space in which to organize these enzymes in the proper organelles. The ultimate unit of integrated structures and functions must necessarily possess a minimal size. As a matter of fact, the diameter of the smallest microorganism capable of independent reproduction is about 5,000 Å.

When one studies the living world, however, one discovers entities able to reproduce their kind which are about 250 Å in diameter. Their volume is therefore 8,000 times smaller than that of the smallest microorganism. These entities are viral particles. They contain proteins and nucleic acid and exhibit a constant and well-defined structure. Viruses are able to reproduce their kind. Yet, the viral particle, as such, is unable to metabolize, to grow, and to undergo binary fusion. Viral multiplication thus poses a certain number of problems.

Viruses can develop only inside a living cell. They are strictly intracellular parasites. A cell infected by a virus very often dies. Sometimes, however, the cell/virus system survives and multiplies. Two systems of order are then intertangled. The viral order is superimposed on the cellular order. As a consequence, the cellular order is perturbed, and the results may be as different as "lysogeny" when bacteria are concerned, or cancer when the mammalian cell is involved.

Various aspects of viral order, viral functions, and cell/virus interactions will be discussed in this chapter.

VIRAL ORDER: THE INFECTIOUS VIRAL PARTICLE, OR VIRION. The most general idea of a viral particle can be derived from the study of one of the simplest and smallest viruses. In order to simplify things, to spare words, and to be modern, the infectious viral particle will be called *virion*, which means a unit of virus, according to recent terminology.

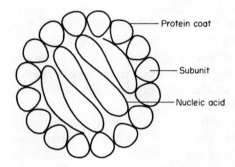

Figure 24. Schematic Representation of a Viral Infectious Particle (Virion).

The genetic material (nucleic acid) is folded and enclosed in a coat or capsid. The capsid is made of subunits, the capsomeres, arranged in an orderly fashion.

The virus of poliomyelitis, the poliovirus, will be taken as a prototype of a virion. This virus has been obtained in a high degree of homogeneity and its chemical constitution established. It has been crystallized and its crystals studied by X-ray diffraction.

The virion is a polyhedron. It is composed of a protein shell enclosing the nucleic acid (Figure 24). X-ray diffraction shows that each virion possesses an icosahedral symmetry. It is built up out of 60 structurally equivalent asymmetric units of approximately 60 Å diameter. If 60 protein subunits of that size are packed together in close contact in a way consistent with icosahedral symmetry, they form a roughly spherical shell of about 300 Å diameter.

This type of structure is clearly seen in electromicroscopic photographs of many viral species. The protein coat of viruses or capsid is actually made up of subunits or capsomeres.

The molecular weight of the virion is approximately 6.7×10^6, of which the protein represents about 62%, the nucleic acid 28%. The protein of the capsid contains about 49,600 amino acids. The nucleic acid is composed of about 5,200 nucleotides.

In the discussion of the code, the conclusion was reached that a sequence of three nucleotides was probably necessary to take care of one amino acid. Therefore, the maximum number of amino acids that can be organized in the viral nucleic acid is 1,700. The genetic material of the virion therefore cannot directly build a molecule composed of 49,600 amino acids, but it can build a number of smaller molecules. Each capsomere is in fact made up of approximately 620 amino acids. The capsid can only be built of subunits, and is in fact built of subunits.

The structure of the viral infectious particle is extraordinary in the sense that it is unique. No other "biological" particle or organelle is yet known which is composed of a large number of asymmetrical subunits exhibiting relations of symmetry. This type of structure seems to be able to form only a viral coat and nothing else.

An entity containing a small number of protein species, let us say one to five, is unable to do much work. It cannot secure energy and cannot synthesize its building blocks. Even if some of the proteins are endowed with a potential enzymatic activity, the virion is metabolically inert. The viral genetic material, in order to express its potentialities, that is, to synthesize the specific viral proteins and to duplicate itself, must necessarily be in an environment where building blocks and energy are provided. These conditions exist only inside a cell, which is the critical living mass.

The essential function of the protein viral coat is to provide a means for the transmission of the genetic material from cell to cell and a protection against the adverse conditions encountered in the outer world.

THE VIRUS. The nucleic acid of a number of viruses has been extracted and purified. If properly handled and if not altered, it may infect cells. The proof of the effectiveness of the infection is the production by the infected cell of a new generation of virions. The virus is reproduced from its genetic material only. At the cellular level, a viral infection is the penetration into a cell of the genetic material of a virus.

The genetic material is RNA in some viruses, DNA in others. A virion never contains both nucleic acids. Every cell, every microorganism without exception, possesses both types of nucleic acid, RNA and DNA. An organized infectious entity possessing only one type of nucleic acid can only be a virus. Moreover, reproduction from the genetic material only is something which neither a cell nor a microorganism can accomplish, and which is an essential and specific feature of viruses. It is clear also that the genetic material of a virus has to possess the information (*a*) for the synthesis of the proteins of the viral coat, and (*b*) for autonomous reproduction.

REMARKS ON THE CONTROL OF VIRAL FUNCTIONS. When a cell is infected by a virus, let us say poliovirus, viral proteins are synthesized, and the genetic material is multiplied. This is the so-called vegetative phase of the viral life cycle. Virions, infective particles, are not produced during the first phase. They appear around the third hour, and thereafter will increase in number. Approximately 6 to 8 hours after the infection each cell contains about 100,000 viral particles, among which only about 500 are infectious. As a result of viral multiplication, the cell is damaged and finally disintegrates.

In a normal, noninfected cell, the synthesis of cellular structures is a well-ordered process. An elaborate system of repression and induction based on a feedback mechanism controls the balanced synthesis of enzymes.

Viruses are sometimes considered as pathological particles of cellular origin. Are viruses, like normal cellular constituents, subject to a regulating system? If a viral regulating system does exist, how do viral and cellular functions interact? The study of bacteriophage should allow us to answer these questions.

Bacteriophage

LIFE-CYCLE OF A VIRULENT BACTERIOPHAGE. The bacteriophage particle is more complicated than the poliovirus. It has a so-called "head" and a so-called "tail" (Figure 25). The head is a hexagonal prism, composed of a ball of DNA surrounded by a protein coat. The tail is a long cylindrical structure, which is composed of (*a*) a contractile outer sheath, (*b*) an internal tube, and (*c*) a tip.

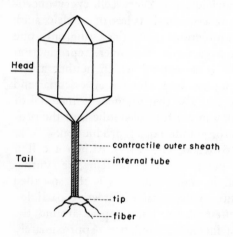

Head

Tail

---- contractile outer sheath
---- internal tube
---- tip
---- fiber

Figure 25. Schematic Representation of a Bacteriophage Particle.

The bacteriophage is not motile. But when the tip of its tail comes into contact with the bacterial wall, the bacteriophage becomes attached to the bacterium (Figure 26). An enzyme present at the extremity of the phage tip attacks the bacterial wall. The external sheath of the tail contracts. The internal tube penetrates through the membrane inside the bacterium. The genetic material is injected through the tube into the bacterial cytoplasm. All this happens within a minute. Then the so-called vegetative phase takes place. The synthesis of phage protein is initiated, and 5 minutes after the infection the genetic material of the bacteriophage starts multiplying. After 12 to 20 minutes, the phage DNA is condensed into a ball, and the subunits of the head are assembled around the ball

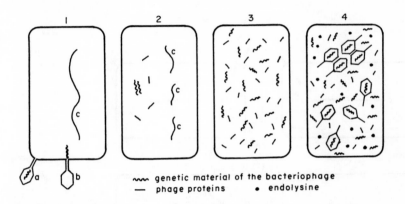

Figure 26. The Life Cycle of a Bacteriophage.

1. Infection: (*a*) the bacteriophage particle has attached onto the receptive bacterium; (*b*) it has injected its genetic material into the bacterium.

2. Beginning of the vegetative phase: Phage proteins are produced, and the autonomous multiplication of the phage genetic material is initiated. The bacterial chromosome c is disintegrating.

3. The bacterial chromosome has disappeared. Its building blocks (nucleic bases) will be incorporated in the phage genetic material. More phage material has been synthesized.

4. The proteins are organized around the folded genetic material, and phage particles are formed. A lytic enzyme (endolysine) will be produced by the vegetative bacteriophage. The bacterial wall will be hydrolyzed and the bacterium will lyse, thus liberating the bacteriophage particles.

of nucleic acid. Finally, by a process that is not understood, the tail appears where it should appear. The infectious particle is formed.

In the meantime, a peculiar phage protein has been produced, the endolysine, which in the particle will be localized at the tip of the tail. This endolysine depolymerizes the mucopolysaccharides of the bacterial wall. The bacterium is lysed and liberates some hundred bacteriophage particles. The so-called "lytic cycle" of the bacterio-phage has been completed. Some bacteriophages, called *virulent* phages, are multiplied only by the lytic cycle. Others, called *temperate* phages, may evolve in two directions.

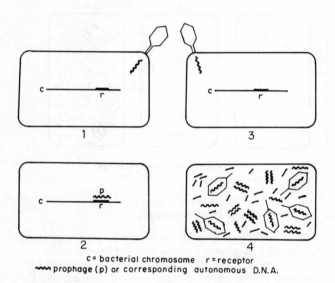

c = bacterial chromosome   r = receptor
~~~ prophage (p) or corresponding autonomous D.N.A.

Figure 27. The Fate of an Infected Nonlysogenic Bacterium.

1 and 2. The genetic material of the phage reaches the specific receptor site (r) of the bacterial chromosome and becomes the prophage (p). The bacterium is lysogenic.

3 and 4. The vegetative phase is started, and infectious particles are produced.

THE TEMPERATE BACTERIOPHAGE; LYSOGENY. After a bacterium has been infected with a temperate phage, the vegetative phase may be started, which culminates in the production of infectious particles and bacterial death. Sometimes, however, the vegetative phase is not started, and the bacterium survives.

The survivors multiply normally (Figure 27). But they are now endowed with a remarkable property. Each surviving bacterium possesses and perpetuates the potentiality of producing bacterio-phage particles in the absence of infection. When this potentiality is not expressed, the bacterium grows and divides. When it is expressed, it dies. The bacteria that perpetuate the possibility of producing bacteriophage in the absence of infection are called *lysogenic*.

THE PROPHAGE. A given bacterial species can be infected by a number of different strains of temperate bacteriophages, let us say A or B, which might differ by a number of properties such as host range, immunological specificity, size, shape, etc. A given bacterium infected and lysogenized by a temperate bacteriophage A will perpetuate the potentiality to produce bacteriophage A. When infected with B, it will perpetuate the potentiality to produce B. The lysogenic bacterium multiplies a specific structure: the prophage (etymologically, "before the phage").

A number of experimental data have led to three essential con-clusions (Figure 28).

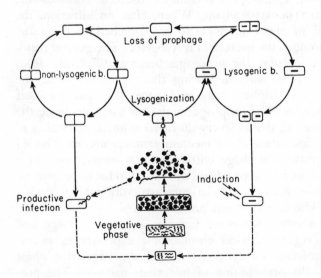

Figure 28. Diagrammatic Representation of Lysogeny (after Lwoff, 1953).

1. The prophage is the genetic material of the bacteriophage. It carries the information for the production of bacteriophage particles.

2. There is only one prophage per bacterial chromosome.

3. A given prophage is always attached to the same site, or locus, of the bacterial chromosome.

THE RECEPTOR. That a given prophage is able to reach and recognize a specific chromosomal site is something strange.

Cytologists know that during a certain phase of the maturation of the sexual cells, a pairing of homologous chromosomes takes place. The two chromosomes stick to each other at their homologous regions. The nature of the forces that intervene in the process is unknown. In any event, it is admitted that the attachment of the viral genetic material on a specific site of the bacterial chromosome is the consequence of a correspondence of structure of the two interacting nucleic acids: the bacterial one and the viral one. This correspondence, whether it is homologous or complementary, is in favor of the hypothesis according to which the genetic material of the phage has, long ago, originated from the bacterial chromosome.

PROPHAGE AND VEGETATIVE PHAGE. When, after an infection, the genetic material of the bacteriophage has attached itself to the bacterial chromosome, the bacterium is lysogenic. The genetic material of the bacteriophage, the prophage, behaves differently from the vegetative genetic material. During the vegetative phase, the viral chromosome multiplies at its own pace. It duplicates itself every 2 or 3 minutes. The prophage duplicates itself alongside the bacterial chromosome, that is, every 20 to 50 minutes, according to the bacterial species, nature of the medium, temperature, etc. During the vegetative phase, the phage chromosome is autonomous. In a lysogenic bacterium, it is, as prophage, submitted to bacterial control. How is it possible that one and the same structure exhibits such a dual behavior? This is one of our problems.

But there is another difference between vegetative phage and prophage. The vegetative viral chromosome expresses its potentialities: viral proteins are synthesized, and the vegetative phase culminates with the organization of infectious particles. The prophage does not express its potentialities: no viral proteins are to be found in a lysogenic bacterium and of course no infectious particles.

A lysogenic bacterium was defined as a bacterium that perpetuates the power to produce bacteriophage in the absence of infection. From time to time, however, the lysogenic bacterium does produce phage, and we have to know why viral functions are sometimes expressed and sometimes not. The study of lysogeny should provide the answer. The simplest hypothesis is that viral functions are not expressed in a lysogenic bacterium because they are blocked by a repressor.

IMMUNITY. A lysogenic bacterium perpetuates the potentiality to produce phage. But thanks to the presence of the prophage the lysogenic bacterium exhibits another property, the so-called immunity. Let us assume that our bacterium has been lysogenized by a temperate bacteriophage A and therefore perpetuates a prophage A. The superinfection by the homologous bacteriophage A does not result in a vegetative phase. The genetic material of the infecting bacteriophage A is injected into the lysogenic bacterium, but it behaves as an inert particle. Viral functions are not expressed. Phage proteins are not produced. Moreover, the genetic material of phage A does not multiply and is diluted out in the course of bacterial multiplication (Figure 29). This immunity is specific. Other types of bacteriophage, let us say B, not genetically related to bacteriophage A can multiply vegetatively, just as if prophage A were not present. Thus, something must be present in the cytoplasm of the lysogenic bacterium carrying prophage A which prevents specifically the vegetative multiplication of the genetic material of phage A. Here again a specific repressor of viral functions can be visualized.

INDUCTION. The probability that a lysogenic population will produce infectious particles varies with the strains from 10^{-2} to 10^{-7} per bacterium per generation. This is the so-called spontaneous phage production, spontaneous because we do not know its cause. In some lysogenic strains, the frequency of spontaneous production cannot be modified. In other strains, the production of bacteriophage can be induced at will in practically all of the population. These strains are called *inducible*.

Inducible lysogenic bacteria are irradiated with a suitable dose of ultraviolet light. The bacteria continue to grow for about 45 minutes. Then within 10 minutes, the bacterial population disappears. All the bacteria have been lysed, and each one has liberated some

100 infectious particles. This is most extraordinary. A bacterium lives in harmony with its prophage. The prophage behaves as if it were a normal bacterial gene. And suddenly, as a result of an irradiation, the vegetative phase of the bacteriophage is initiated, and the

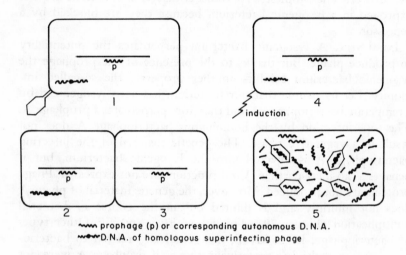

prophage (p) or corresponding autonomous D.N.A.
D.N.A. of homologous superinfecting phage

Figure 29. Immunity.

1–3. The lysogenic bacterium is superinfected with a mutant of the homologous phage. The genetic material of the superinfecting phage does not initiate the vegetative phase, does not divide, and is diluted out at each division. One of the daughter bacteria (3) contains only the prophage.

4–5. The superinfected bacterium is induced, for example, by an irradiation with ultraviolet light. The vegetative phase of both prophages and the superinfecting phage are initiated, and infectious particles of both types will be produced.

lysogenic bacterium produces bacteriophage and dies. If, previous to the irradiation, the lysogenic bacterium has been infected with a mutant of the homologous phage toward which the bacterium is immune, the mutant will develop together with the prophage. The problem of the control of viral development is thus posed in the most dramatic way.

INDUCING AGENTS. Ultraviolet light has an inducing effect but is not the only inducer. A number of physical or chemical agents are also inducers — among them, X rays, gamma rays, nitrogen mustard, organic peroxides, epoxides, and ethylenimines. All these agents are known to be mutagenic and oncogenic, that is, cancer-inducing. The fact that inducing agents are mutagenic is not a great help: induction of a lysogenic bacterium is not homologous to a mutation. But the fact that inducing agents are able to initiate malignant growth is rather exciting. Perhaps induction will help us to understand cancer, but the reverse is certainly not true. Anyhow, the theory is that the inducing agents depress or block the synthesis of the repressor. As a consequence, the level of the repressor decreases below a given threshold. Since the prophage is no longer repressed, the vegetative phase is initiated.

A noninducible prophage could be a prophage which manufactures more repressor, or a more stable repressor, or which has a greater affinity for the repressor. This problem will be discussed later.

ZYGOTIC INDUCTION. The prophage λ of *Escherichia coli* K12 is located on the bacterial chromosome close to one of the genes controlling the utilization of galactose, which enters into the female at about the 25th minute after conjugation.

If both male and female are lysogenic, nothing happens after conjugation, a fact that is worth while noticing. If only the female is lysogenic, nothing happens either. But if a lysogenic male mates with a nonlysogenic female, things are quite different (Figure 30). As soon as the prophage attached to the chromosome of the lysogenic male has penetrated into the nonlysogenic female, the vegetative phase is initiated, bacteriophage particles are produced, and the female is lysed. Thus, phage development is induced when, as a result of conjugation or zygosis, an inducible prophage penetrates into a nonlysogenic cytoplasm. This is *zygotic induction*.

These data are consistent with the hypothesis that in the lysogenic male bacterium the expression of the viral functions is blocked by a cytoplasmic repressor. When the prophage of the lysogenic male enters the nonlysogenic female, repression ceases because the cytoplasm of the female is devoid of repressor, and viral functions are expressed. How could the repressor act? The antibiotic chloramphenicol is known to block the synthesis of proteins. If bacterial

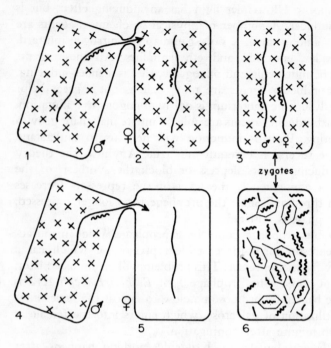

∿ phage D.N.A. — phage proteins ◴ repressor

Figure 30. Prophage during Bacterial Recombination.

Upper row: The lysogenic male (1) (repressor present) injects its chromosome and prophage into the lysogenic female (2) (repressor present). The vegetative phase is not initiated.

Lower row: The lysogenic male (4) (repressor present) injects its chromosome and prophage in a nonlysogenic female (no repressor). The vegetative phase is initiated: this is zygotic induction.

conjugation takes place in the presence of chloramphenicol, zygotic induction does not take place in a large fraction of the zygotes. It could be that the viral function necessary for the onset of the vegetative phase is the synthesis of a protein. If this interpretation is correct, it should be applied to infection and lysogenization.

INFECTION AND LYSOGENIZATION. A nonlysogenic bacterium infected by a temperate phage may either produce infectious particles and be lysed, or become lysogenic. The outcome of the infection depends on the genetic constitution of the temperate bacteriophage. But with a given temperate bacteriophage, the behavior of the bacterium/phage system, and the fate of the bacterium, are controlled by extrinsic factors.

The fraction of the infected bacteria that will be lysogenized varies effectively from less than 1% to more than 99%. A high temperature (40°C.) favors the establishment of the lytic cycle, whereas a low temperature (20°C.) acts in favor of lysogenization (Figure 31).

The low or high temperature acts only during the first 7 minutes after infection. After the seventh minute the decision is made and cannot be modified. Something irreversible has happened. Thus, the experimental data point toward the conclusion that the response of the infected bacterium depends on a primary determining event. What is this event?

It was found that antibiotics which block protein synthesis, such as chloramphenicol, favor the lysogenic response. The hypothesis is that the first event can be the synthesis either of a protein or of something else, namely, a repressor. If a protein is produced first, the vegetative phase is initiated, and the process is irreversible from then on. More proteins are synthesized, the viral DNA is duplicated, and finally infectious particles are produced. If a repressor is produced first, the expression of the viral potentialities is blocked. Proteins cannot be synthesized, and the autonomous cytoplasmic viral DNA is unable to duplicate itself. But, thanks to the correspondence of structure with a given chromosomal locus, the viral DNA attaches itself to this receptor site. It is now a prophage. The prophage multiplies; later on, we shall try to understand why it does. It continues to produce the repressor, and the bacterium is now lysogenic. The repressor hypothesis needs of course to be reinforced, and it will be reinforced by the study of viral mutants.

MUTATIONS AFFECTING INDUCIBILITY. The genetic material of a bacteriophage, like any other genetic material, may undergo mutations. The wild-type λ ind+ is inducible with ultraviolet light. A mutant ind− was discovered which had lost its original inducibility

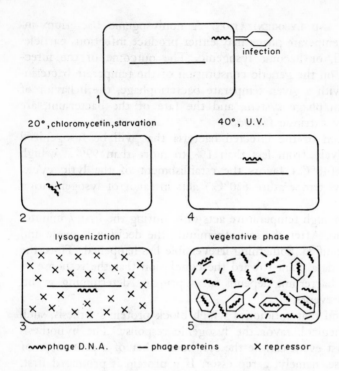

Figure 31. The Fate of the Infected Bacterium.

The nonlysogenic bacterium is infected:

1-3: at low temperature (20°C.) in the presence of chloramphenicol, or in bacteria deprived of food, the first activity of the genetic material of the repressor. As a consequence the synthesis of phage protein is repressed, the vegetative phase is not initiated, and the genetic material of the phage reaches its chromosomal locus and becomes a prophage.

4-5: at high temperature (40°C.), or in a bacterium irradiated with ultra-violet rays. The first activity of the genetic material of the phage is the synthesis of a protein. The vegetative phase is initiated, and infectious particles are produced.

with ultraviolet light, although all other characters of the mutant were the same as those of the original strain. The mutant not induci-ble with ultraviolet light is, however, sensitive to zygotic induction. Double lysogenic strains can be obtained that carry two prophages λ:

the inducible one, and the noninducible one. When these strains are irradiated with ultraviolet light, none of the bacteriophages develop. In the presence of λ ind$^-$, the phage λ ind$^+$ cannot be induced. The noninductive mutation λ ind$^-$ is dominant.

When a bacterium carrying prophage λ ind$^+$ is irradiated with ultraviolet light, it is induced and will produce phage (Table V).

Table V. Variation of Inducibility.

	Inducibility		Interpretations	
	by ultraviolet light	zygotic	Repressor	
			lability	affinity for operator
Inducible	+	+	+ + +	+
Semi-inducible	0	+	+ +	+ +
Noninducible	0	0	+	+ + +

The effect of ultraviolet light can be suppressed by superinfection with the noninducible λ phage. All these data are compatible with the hypothesis that the noninducible bacteriophage λ ind$^-$ either produces more repressor than the wild type or produces an altered repressor that could, for example, be more stable. It could also produce a repressor possessing a higher affinity for the hypothetical operator gene of the bacteriophage.

MUTATIONS AFFECTING VIRULENCE. One of the characteristics of phage λ is its ability to lysogenize. It is, by definition, a temperate bacteriophage. Some mutations of λ affect the possibility to lysogenize (Table VI). The mutants are unable to lysogenize, but they are still sensitive to the repressor, for they do not develop in a lysogenic λ. It is tempting to suppose that these mutants have lost the property to produce a repressor. This type of phage can finally give rise to a more extreme mutant type of virulent phage. These mutants are unable to lysogenize, but in contrast to their ancestor, they are able to develop in a lysogenic bacterium carrying pro-

Table VI. Mutations Affecting the Life Cycle.

	Bacteriophage		
	Normal temperate	"Clear" mutants	Virulent mutants
Ability to lysogenize	+	0	0
Ability to develop in a lysogenic bacterium	0	0	+
Repressor production of	+	0	0
Repressor sensitivity to	+	+	0

phage λ. This means that they have become *insensitive to the repressor* produced by phage λ.

It should be recalled here that immunity in a lysogenic bacterium is specific. A bacterium carrying prophage A is immune toward the superinfecting phage A but not toward a nongenetically related phage B. The repressor is specific. And as it controls the expression or activity of the viral nucleic acid, it must be assumed that it has to establish with it some sort of physical relation. The most likely hypothesis is that the specific repressor attaches itself onto a specific spot of the viral chromosome. In the evolution of a temperate bacteriophage toward virulence, two steps have thus been recognized. The first is the loss of the ability to produce a repressor. The second is the loss of the sensitivity to the repressor. From a temperate phage, a virulent one has been obtained. It is unable to lysogenize and can only multiply vegetatively, just like the most virulent phages encountered in nature.

MUTATIONS AFFECTING THE VEGETATIVE PHASE. In a normal lysogenic population, any bacterium is potentially able to produce bacteriophage, and it will produce bacteriophage and lyse if induced. In some strains of lysogenic bacteria, all bacteria lyse after induction, but only one out of 10^{-5} will produce bacteriophage. Absence of bacteriophage production is due to a genetic defect of the prophage. Defective lysogenics belong to different categories (Table VII).

Some are able to manufacture the proteins of the phage. In others, the synthesis of one or more of these proteins is impossible, and the genetic material of the phage, so far as is known, is not multiplied.

It seems as though the vegetative phase could be characterized by a sequence of events. Each event has to be completed so that the following one can be initiated. And apparently, in the absence of protein synthesis, the chromosome of the defective bacteriophage

Table VII. Defective Prophages.

	1	2	3	4	5
Autonomous (vegetative) multiplication of the genome	+	+	0	0	0
Synthesis of phage protein H	+	+	+	+	0
Synthesis of endolysine	+	+	+	0	+
Production of infective particles	+	0	0	0	0

is unable to multiply vegetatively. The autonomous multiplication of the viral genetic material seems to depend on the expression of a certain number of viral functions, perhaps on a sequence of functions.

In a defective prophage, the capacity to multiply as an autonomous unit may be altered. But the genetic alteration does not affect the ability to multiply as prophage, that is, as an integrated unit. When it is attached to the bacterial chromosome, the genetic material of the defective phage is submitted to the bacterial system of control and multiplies despite its genetic defects that affect only autonomous multiplication.

Let us recall that in a normal lysogenic bacterium the expression of the viral functions of the prophage is repressed. The hypothetical repressor prevents also the expression of the functions of superinfecting homologous bacteriophage. As a consequence, the genetic material is unable to multiply autonomously.

In a lysogenic strain, the initiation of the vegetative phase and the autonomous replication of the viral genetic material can take place only if the genetic material of the phage is no longer exposed to the repressor.

1. This happens when the prophage of the lysogenic male enters a nonlysogenic female where no repressor is present.

2. This happens also if the repressor balance is upset by inducing agents such as ultraviolet light.

Let me repeat that the virulent mutants of a temperate phage are unable to produce a repressor and are insensitive to the repressor produced by the original prophage. They develop despite the presence of a repressor, and they produce the proteins necessary for the onset of the vegetative phase of their own life cycle.

It has been admitted that the prophage does not enter the vegetative phase because it is unable to produce some specific protein. If this hypothesis corresponds to the facts, the virulent mutant, which does multiply and which does produce these proteins, should induce the vegetative development of the prophage. If a lysogenic bacterium is infected with a virulent phage genetically related to the prophage, the homologous prophage enters the vegetative phase. All the experimental data are thus in agreement with the hypothesis that autonomous multiplication of a phage requires the manufacture of a protein. The synthesis of this protein may be blocked by a specific repressor.

Interactions of Cellular and Viral Functions

CELLULAR CONTROL OF VIRAL REPRODUCTION. The most important aspect of the reproduction of the viral genetic material has not yet been discussed. In a lysogenic bacterium, the chromosome of the superinfecting bacteriophage does not multiply, whereas the prophage multiplies, whether it is attached to the chromosome or to an episome such as the sexual F factor (Figure 32).

Thus, the behavior of two structurally identical viral chromosomes might be different. Their properties seem to be controlled by their position in the bacterium. Position is the fourth dimension of the prophage.

Moreover, the prophage is duplicated in harmony with the

cellular organelle to which it is attached; that is, one duplication occurs every 20 to 50 minutes. The prophage is obviously subject to the system that controls the duplication of the bacterial chromosome. What is this system? As a matter of fact, the first question is: Does such a system exist?

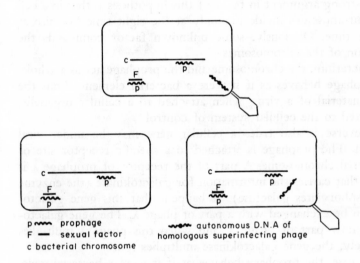

p ~~~ prophage
F — sexual factor
c bacterial chromosome
~•~ autonomous D.N.A of homologous superinfecting phage

Figure 32. Integrated and Nonintegrated Genetic Material.

The lysogenic bacterium carries two prophages: one of them is attached to the bacterial chromosome, the other to the fertilizing factor or sexual factor (F). It is infected by a mutant of the homologous phage. Since the lysogenic bacteria is immune, the vegetative phase is not initiated. The autonomous genetic material of the superinfecting phage does not multiply, whereas both integrated phage genetic materials do divide.

In a normal cell, in a normal microorganism, the multiplication of the chromosome is in harmony with the growth of the cell and its division. When things proceed normally, no problem is posed. If the replication of a cellular chromosome should be impaired, the cell would die. A lethal defect of an indispensable cellular organelle obviously cannot be perpetuated. But such a lethal defect can exist and persist in a prophage which is reproduced as nucleic acid and which can be perpetuated without expressing its potentialities.

The study of the behavior of the defective prophage after induction has revealed the existence of a set of functions controlling the duplication of the viral nucleic acid. The existence of such functions for the duplication of the cellular chromosome can only be postulated. A strong argument in favor of this hypothesis is that in a cell all the chromosomes divide not only at the right time but also at the same time. Obviously, some unknown factor commands the duplication of the chromosomes.

In a bacterium, the chromosome and the prophage act as a whole. The prophage behaves as if it were a bacterial element. Thus the genetic material of a virus, when attached to a cellular organelle, is submitted to the cellular system of control.

The reverse is also true: a cellular gene may be under viral command. The prophage is attached to a specific receptor site of the bacterial chromosome. A part of the receptor of prophage λ is the gene that carries the information for galactokinase (the enzyme that phosphorylates galactose). It happens that this gene galactokinase can be exchanged with a part of phage λ. The gene galactokinase is now part of phage λ, and when this phage λ multiplies vegetatively, the gene galactokinase multiplies too.

In one case, the prophage behaves as if it were a bacterial gene. In the other case, a bacterial gene behaves as if it were a viral gene. This probably means that a given chromosome, whether cellular or viral, and the "foreign" nucleic acid it may carry constitute a unit and behave as a whole, so far as replication is concerned.

The study of the functional order, of the induction and repression of enzyme synthesis, has revealed a different situation: the various individual systems controlling enzyme synthesis are independent in the sense that one may be blocked while the others are working. The enzymes for tryptophan synthesis may be produced while those for methionine synthesis are repressed. Are viruses able to take command of cellular functions? The reader realizes of course that the question would not be posed if a positive answer could not be provided.

VIRAL CONTROL OF CELLULAR FUNCTIONS. A nonlysogenic *Salmonella* produces a given somatic antigen 10. If lysogenized with a given phage ε 15, it stops producing the antigen 10, and in turn produces another antigen 15. The mechanism by which prophage 15 controls the synthesis of a bacterial antigen is still a mystery.

A much more fascinating situation has been disclosed with galactokinase. A short digression is necessary here. The gene galactokinase and the prophage λ are closely linked. Both may be attached to the sexual factor F, and thus transferred from the male to the female. If the partners are properly selected, a large variety of heterozygotes may be obtained. It happens that in the absence of an inducer the bacteria contain only a small amount of galactokinase. A marked synthesis of the enzyme takes place only when an inducer is present. But when phage λ develops vegetatively, either as a result of an infection or as a consequence of an induction, then the enzyme galactokinase is synthesized in large amounts in the absence of an inducer. This synthesis takes place only when the gene and the phage are in position *cis* (when they are part of the same structure), and not in position *trans* (when they are in different structures).

Things happen here as if the bacterial gene were obeying some viral mechanism of control, perhaps a viral operator. Thus a virus may be subject to the control system of a bacterium, and a bacterial gene to the control system of a virus, both for replication and for expression.

VIRAL AND NONVIRAL DISEASES. When a defective lysogenic bacterium is induced, the defective prophage is derepressed. An abnormal vegetative phase is initiated. Bacteriophage particles are not produced, but the bacterium nevertheless dies. The disease is not the result of an infection, and infectious particles have not been formed. Strictly speaking, the disease is not viral. The defective prophage possesses some of the normal viral genes but behaves as a potential lethal gene (Table VIII). A few hereditary, nonviral diseases of bacteria are known which are controlled not by a defective prophage but by genetic structures that have to be visualized as bacterial genes, potentially lethal genes. Between these hereditary diseases and viral diseases, an almost complete series of intermediary steps has been disclosed, and the hypothesis that the genetic material of viruses has evolved from cellular genes is currently admitted.

VIRUSES AND CANCER. Thus a virus may be multiplied as genetic

Table VIII. Genes and Viruses.

	Sensitivity to a system of repression	Lethality of expression	Information for autonomous multiplication	Possibility of forming infective particles
Inductive gene	+	0	0	0
Pathological gene	+	+	0	0
Defective prophage	+	+	0	0
	+	+	+	0
Temperate phage	+	+	+	+
Virulent phage	0	+	+	+

material when it is in the form of a provirus. The expressions of the viral functions are then blocked, that is, repressed, and the lysogenic bacterium grows and multiplies. But the prophage is present, a self-perpetuating sword of Damocles. When it is derepressed, the functions for its autonomous reproduction are set free: the vegetative phase is initiated, and the bacterium is killed.

As a consequence of the presence of the prophage, the lysogenic bacterium necessarily differs from the nonlysogenic one. The fact that lysogenic bacteria are frequently found in nature seems to indicate that the prophage might sometimes be useful, partly perhaps because it confers immunity on the bacterium. But the bacterium is an independent unit. A provirus may alter its competitive value and thus modify the outcome of a competition, but the bacterium/ provirus system, considered in itself, is perfectly viable. This should be true also for an animal cell/virus system. However, the bacterium is an organism, an independent system, whereas the animal cell is a dependent part of an organism.

Some animal viruses generally kill the cell they infect. This is the case for the agents of acute diseases such as poliomyelitis, smallpox, and yellow fever. These viruses are comparable to the virulent phages. Other animal viruses behave like the temperate phages. This is true especially of oncogenic viruses, the viruses responsible for cancer. The infected cell is sometimes killed; it sometimes survives. When it survives, it is endowed with the potentiality for producing virus in the absence of infection; it is immune to super-infection. It may also be modified in its morphology and physiology. But there is something more: the animal cell/virus system is now malignant. Injected into an animal, it multiplies and kills its host. The original cell was normal, subject to the factors that control cell reproduction. The transformed cell has lost its sensitivity to these yet-unknown factors. Whether or not the genetic material of the virus multiplies autonomously as provirus is not yet known. It could be one way or the other, according to the nature of the cell and of the virus. At least one thing is certain. In some of the animal cell/oncogenic virus systems, viral functions are repressed. Viral antigens and infectious particles are not produced. When, as a result of an alteration of the cell's environment, viral functions are derepressed, viral antigens and viral particles are produced. The cancer problem is not solved so far; the nature of the cellular modi-fication which is due to the virus or provirus and responsible for malignancy is still unknown. Yet it is interesting to consider the animal cell/provirus system. As already stated, the bacterium is an organism, the normal cell a dependent part of an organism. The malignant cell behaves in the animal as if it were independent, and the host is killed.

A virus, in order to be oncogenic, must not kill the cell it infects. And a low virulence for the cell may mean a high degree of patho-genicity for the animal. It is, however, not the oncogenic virus itself that kills the cancerous animal but the cell/virus system, the cell modified by the virus. The fact that specific repressors are known to control some viral functions opens a new way of approach to the problem of oncogenic viruses.

According to the Platonic concept, all things originate in their opposites. Darkness comes from light, cold from heat, pleasure from pain. Biological order had its origin in primitive disorder. But if the question is asked: What can originate from order? the only possible answer is disorder.

It is clear that the superposition of two types of structural order may be responsible for functional disorder. Structures and functions are complementary in normal processes as well as in pathological processes. Biological disorder is the complementary aspect of biological order.

REFERENCES

Adams, M. H. (1959). *Bacteriophages*. Interscience Publishers, New York.

Burnet, F. M., and Stanley, W. M., eds. (1959). *The Viruses — Biochemical, Biological, and Biophysical Properties*, Volume I. Academic Press, New York.

Finch, J. T., and Klug, A. (1959). Structure of poliomyelitis virus. *Nature, 183,* 1709–1714.

Jacob, F. (1958–1959). Genetic control of viral functions. *The Harvey Lectures,* series *54,* 1–39. Academic Press, New York.

Luria, S. E. (1953). *General Virology*. John Wiley & Sons, New York.

Lwoff, A. (1954–1955). Control and interrelations of metabolic and viral diseases of bacteria. *The Harvey Lectures,* series *50,* 92–111. Academic Press, New York.

Wollman, E. L., and Jacob, F. (1959). La sexualité des bactéries. *Monographies de l'Institut Pasteur,* pp. 43–59. Masson, Paris.

Wollman, E. L., and Jacob, F. (1959). Lysogeny, transduction and cancer genesis. In *Genetics and Cancer*, pp. 43–59. University of Texas Press, Austin.

VI. BIOLOGICAL ORDER AND ENTROPY

Sources of Energy

An organism is a machine. In order to operate, a machine has to be fed something, for example coal. It is not coal, however, that causes the steam engine to operate, but the combustion of coal.

The living machine, in order to operate, must also be fed. It needs energy. When the organism possesses chlorophyll, the source of energy is light. When the organism is devoid of chlorophyll, the energy is provided by the chemical bonds of the food. The organism, in this case, burns more-or-less complex substances: organic compounds such as sugars or amino acids, or mineral compounds such as hydrogen sulfide, carbon monoxide, or even hydrogen.

The organism performs oxidoreductions. The general equation may be written:

$$AH_2 \quad + \quad B \quad \longrightarrow \quad A \quad + \quad BH_2$$

hydrogen donor   hydrogen acceptor   oxidized   reduced
(reduced state)   (oxidized state)   donor   acceptor

If, for example, the hydrogen acceptor is oxygen, the reaction is

$$AH_2 + \tfrac{1}{2} O_2 \longrightarrow A + H_2O$$

This is respiration.

Metabolism and syntheses consist essentially in the mobilization of the energy of the chemical bonds of the food. Max Delbrück has described an organism as a system of flux equilibrium which takes matter and energy from its environment.

Equations

In any chemical reaction, one has to distinguish between the total heat of reactions ($-\Delta H$) and the free energy of reactions ($-\Delta F$). The free energy F gives a measure of the maximum amount of work obtainable.

In the reaction:

$$CH_4 + 2O_2 \longrightarrow CO_2 + 2H_2O$$

$$\text{gas} \qquad \text{gas} \qquad \text{gas} \qquad \text{liquid}$$

$-\Delta H = 212,600$ calories
$-\Delta F = 194,600$ calories

In most biological reactions, only a small fraction of the total heat is available for work. The combustion of food necessarily produces heat.

Now, living beings exhibit a peculiar feature which is not found in inanimate machines. Whereas a machine can maintain its structure even if it does not work, an organism is unable to do so, at least at biological temperatures. In an organism, whether or not extrinsic food is available, the enzymes responsible for oxidation are working. These enzymes perform their task, which consists in oxidizing something. If the organism is not provided with an oxidizable reduced compound, then it first burns its reserves, fat and sugar. Then it burns its proteins, that is, destroys its noble substance; and then it ultimately dies. Thus the organism has to be fed, even if does not perform syntheses.

The equation of the resting organism may be written:

$$\text{Organism} + \text{food} \longrightarrow \text{organism} + \text{waste} + \text{heat}$$

Energy is partly dissipated as heat. The other part corresponds to protoplasmic movements, for all the constituent parts of a cell are constantly moving.

Thus the mere maintenance of biological order involves a degradation of energy. But one essential feature of life is reproduction, and the general equation of life may be written:

$$(\text{Organism})_1 + \text{food} \longrightarrow (\text{organism})_2 + \text{waste} + \text{heat}$$

Reproduction as well as maintenance involves a degradation of energy. But during reproduction two organisms have been produced out of one. Order has increased.

Entropy is a measure of atomic disorder. An increase of disorder corresponds to an increase of entropy, and an increase of order to a decrease of entropy. As our subject is biological order, we have to consider the production or reproduction of order in its most general aspect, namely, from a thermodynamical viewpoint.

Entropy

Physicists know that every isolated system changes in such a way as to approach a definite state of rest. This state of rest is a state of equilibrium. It corresponds not to a loss but to a degradation of energy. The entropic change during such an irreversible process is the difference between the entropy at the end and the entropy at the beginning. The measure of entropy is a measure of a difference between an initial and a final state.

The value of entropy is given by the formula:

$$\text{Entropy} = k \log D$$

where k is the Boltzmann constant and D is the measure of the atomic disorder. The state of rest which an isolated system tends to reach corresponds to a maximum entropy, that is, to a maximum disorder.

Now entropy, being a measure of disorder, is related to probability. In a closed system evolving from a less probable to a more probable state, the probability increases, and so does entropy. The relation between entropy and probability is given by the Boltzmann–Planck formula:

$$S = k \ln P$$

where S is the entropy, k the Boltzmann constant expressed in ergs per degree centigrade, that is, 1.38×10^{-16}, and P the number of "elementary complexions." "Elementary complexions" correspond to the "discrete configurations," that is, to the jumps of the atomic system from one metastable structure to another.

Thus, entropy is a measure of atomic disorder. Physicists have found it convenient to have an expression for its reverse, that is, the degree of atomic order or the availability for work. This negative entropy, "negentropy," represents the *quality* or *grade* of energy. And we may admit with Schrödinger that if D is a measure of atomic disorder, its reciprocal $1/D$ will be a measure of atomic order.

If entropy $S = k \log D$, negative entropy or negentropy $N = k \log 1/D$.

Life and Entropy

A system is said to be closed when it does not carry on exchanges of matter with its surroundings. A closed system is said to be isolated when it does not interact in any way with its surroundings. An organism separated from its surroundings will soon die, and is therefore an abstraction. A living system cannot be closed, nor *a fortiori* isolated, like the systems studied by physicists.

It should be clear that the live system under consideration is the organism plus a reasonable — that is, unlimited — supply of food.

Let us now consider the equation of reproduction:

$$(\text{Organism})_1 + \text{food} \longrightarrow (\text{organism})_2 + \text{waste} + \text{heat}$$

The organism has synthesized its building blocks — its essential metabolites, nucleic bases, and amino acids — and has organized them into specific macromolecules. As a result of the functioning of the living machine, work has been produced and energy has been degraded. As already stated, order has increased. Increase of order corresponds to a decrease of entropy. Thus, as a result of reproduction, entropy has decreased. Has the over-all entropy of the system represented in the equation for metabolism and reproduction increased or decreased? To answer the question, we have to measure the decrease of entropy corresponding to the increase of order. How can we measure the atomic order, that is, the negative entropy in a living organism?

Information and Negentropy

This brings us to the negentropy principle of information. What is information? We shall follow Brillouin's analysis. One considers a problem involving a certain number of possible answers when no information is available. When some information is gained, then the number of possible answers is reduced, and "complete information" means only one possible answer. Information is a function of the ratio of possible answers before and after.

The initial situation is

$$I_0 = 0$$

with P_0 probable or possible outcomes.

The final situation is

$$I_1 \neq 0$$

with $P_1 = 1$, that is to say, one single outcome selected.

The information I is

$$I_1 = K \ln P_0$$

This definition of information is based on scarcity. The lower the probability, the higher the scarcity and the higher the information.

In 1929, Leo Szilard discovered the existence of a connection between information and entropy. And the demonstration has been provided that information corresponds to negative entropy.

The similarity between the two formulas of entropy

$$S = k \ln P$$

and information

$$I_1 = K \ln P_0$$

is obvious. If the Boltzmann constant is used, information is measured in entropy units:

$$I_1 = 1.38 \times 10^{-16} \ln P_0$$

The information of any specific organization can thus be expressed in entropy units. For example, the negentropy of a telephone network with 10^8 subscribers can be calculated to be 4×10^{-7}.

What is the information, that is, the negentropy, of an organism? This is, as pointed out by Brillouin in his classical book, an unexplored field of research.

The Negentropy of
Biological Organization

Physicists know that in a machine the structural negentropy represents the information or organization of the machine. How can we visualize the structural negentropy of an organism or of a cell? Each species of macromolecule, whether it is a polysaccharide, a protein, or a nucleic acid, is part of the organization of the living machine. One could consider that the negentropy of an organism is the sum of the negentropy of its specific macromolecules. But the problem can be simplified.

The organization of all the macromolecules of an organism has its origin in the organization of the hereditary material, which is nucleic acid. In the bacterium *Escherichia coli*, the hereditary material is composed of 10^7 nucleic bases belonging to 4 categories organized in a given sequence. Since this is so, we can calculate the number of possible arrangements of the 10^7 units. It is 4^{10^7}.

For the calculation of the information of our bacterium, we have assumed that at the origin there were 4^{10^7} possible outcomes, and that today there is only one, selected from among a large number of probabilities.

If we apply the formula

$$I = 1.38 \times 10^{-16} \ln P_0$$

it follows that

$$I = 1.38 \times 10^{-16} \ln 4^{10^7}$$

The structural negentropy of the bacterium *Escherichia coli* is around 2×10^{-9} entropy units, that is, ergs/°C.

This figure was obtained by considering only the genetic material. But an organism is much more than its genetic material. It contains a few thousand enzymes and a large number of other specific macromolecules. This organization should perhaps be considered also in the calculation of the amount of information. But the problem of physical entropy is even more complicated. The study of the functional order has revealed a very high degree of nonstructural, functional coupling between the active units of a cell. And Linschitz has proposed that this type of organization should also be taken into account in the calculation of what he calls a "biological negentropy." This is certainly a very pertinent suggestion. I would like to illustrate this point by an example. As a result of an accident, one nucleic base of the genetic material is sometimes replaced by another. This alteration may cause the death of the organism. If, for example, one given molecule of guanine in a given gene is replaced by a molecule of adenine, the information, the structural negentropy of the system, is the same. For the physicist, even if the mutation is lethal, nothing has changed: the content in negentropy has remained the same. But the mutation being lethal, the altered organism is now unable to function normally and to reproduce. It has ceased to be alive. As a consequence of the introduction of the genetic material of a virus, the negentropy of a cell/virus system is greater than the negentropy of the normal, original, noninfected cell. But the infected cell will die; that is, its information will be destroyed.

The value of the negentropy obviously does not give a measure of the efficiency of the system. The living organism is not only an improbable system but a system fitted for certain functions. Low probability and value are not synonymous. Brillouin has proposed a generalized negentropy principle that would take into account the value of the organization or information. This corresponds to a radical development and a broad extension of the notion of entropy and to something quite different from the classical physical concept.

The biologist feels that the functional order is an essential part of the living system. It is clear, however, that this functional order cannot be measured in terms of entropy units, and is meaningless from a purely thermodynamical point of view. And it happens, as will be seen next, that the term "information" has for the biologist a different sense than for the physicist.

Remarks on "Genetic Information"

The synthesis of a given specific protein is under the control of nucleic acid. Nucleic acid therefore contains the blueprint for the orderly assemblage of amino acids into proteins, that is, for the production with a probability 1 of a given specific structure. The blueprint is called genetic information, and this is most regrettable.

In a machine, the organization represents information, or structural negative entropy. In an organism, the hereditary organization has every right to be called information.

Physicists know that the value of a message is not taken into account in the measure of the information. A theorem by Einstein or a random assemblage of letters both contain the same information, provided the number of letters is the same. This should apply to genetic information. For the physicist, all the genes, provided they contain the same number of bases, have the same information, that is, the same content, which is negative entropy. But the biologist knows that each gene is different from every other, for each gene controls the synthesis of one given specific protein. The biologist currently speaks of information for the synthesis of a given enzyme. The concept of probability has disappeared, and the idea of quality, the specific value, is included in the biological concept of genetic information.

The gene as a machine, or organization, contains information that is negative entropy. But, for the biologist, "genetic information" refers to a given actual structure or order of the hereditary material and not to the negative entropy of this structure. Both the physicist and the biologist should be well aware of this situation.

Entropy and Evolution

When functional order is considered, it appears that the biological order is considerably greater than the figure calculated by considering only the probability of the base sequence in the hereditary material. But there is something more, for evolution must be also taken into account.

It is believed that life originated some 3×10^9 years ago and that the organisms existing today are the consequence of a long evolution. Nothing positive is known about the origin of life, and our position is, therefore, in a sense, privileged. Yet, for very good reasons, biologists say that at the beginning there were organic molecules. These were formed as a result of the action of ultraviolet light on simple inorganic compounds. The organic molecules then assembled on some substrate such as colloidal clay, and an organic gel endowed with catalytic properties eventually appeared. As a result of a large number of experiments, the catalytic "metabolizing" gel gave rise to something able to reproduce itself. This was the first organism, certainly very different from any current living being. The first organism in turn started performing experiments, producing new and better organisms that outgrew the original prototype. As a result, a large number of species were selected, which today constitute the living world.

The present biological order includes the historical experience of the organism acquired during its evolution. And it is because it includes evolution that it is so highly improbable. Everything unfit has been eliminated. A large number of experiments, at the same time structural and functional, have been performed. They necessarily correspond to an increase of entropy. The organization of the actually living systems has been acquired at the expense of an increase of entropy. This increase should be taken into account in any calculation of the negative entropy of the organism.

Let us consider again the equation

$$(\text{Organism})_1 + \text{food} \longrightarrow (\text{organism})_2 + \text{waste} + \text{heat}$$

The structural negentropy N, due to the production of two organisms out of one, has doubled at the expense of an increase of entropy S, due to the degradation of energy. Is ΔN smaller or larger than ΔS? In other words, has the over-all entropy decreased or increased? The system organism plus food might be visualized as a closed system but certainly not as an isolated system. When an organism metabolizes, heat is excreted, and as a result the entropy of the surrounding world is increased. The living system considered on a world-wide scale cannot contradict the second principle, despite the fact that it contains and reproduces structural negative entropy and a very remarkable functional order.

The Source of Orderliness

In his remarkable book *What Is Life*, Schrödinger states that everything that is going on in nature means an increase of entropy and that the living being continuously increases its entropy, that is, produces positive entropy, thus approaching the state of maximum entropy, which is death. This is certainly all right. The organism can remain alive, says Schrödinger, only by continuously drawing negative entropy from its environment. Negative entropy is, according to Schrödinger, "something very positive," that is, a measure of order.

The organism, according to Schrödinger, maintains its order by "sucking orderliness" from its environment. For the animal, the sources of orderliness are more-or-less complex organic compounds; for the plant, the source of orderliness is the sunlight. This type of reasoning has been endorsed by Brillouin, who writes, "If a living organism needs food, it is only for the negentropy which it can get from it and which is needed to make up for the losses due to mechanical work done, or simple degradation processes in the living system. Energy contained in food does not really matter, since energy is conserved and never gets lost, but negentropy is the important matter."

The statements concerning negative entropy, or orderliness, as the real fuel for the maintenance of life should be examined from a biological point of view and also from a physical point of view.

A steam engine is kept working by the combustion of coal. The combustion of coal is the source of movement of the machine; it is not the source of the structure. I know that the formula "the organism feeds on negative entropy" has been applied to the maintenance of the living system. But maintenance of the organism — that is, maintenance of biological order — is only one aspect of life, reproduction being the other. It has been known for a long time that only an organism can give rise to an organism. Schrödinger himself has pointed out very pertinently that the characteristic of life is the production of order from order. The only source of biological order is biological order. Now, maintenance as well as reproduction of biological order both depend on the same process, namely, metabolism, which is correlative to an increase of entropy. Because biological order, or organization, just like information, can be expressed in terms of negentropy, such statements as "The organism remains alive by sucking orderliness from its environment," even when it applies only to maintenance, might be misleading.

The organism, if it wants to work, has to burn something, just as the steam engine does. It might burn sugar, for example. But it is clear that what is important in the molecule of sugar is not the structural negentropy of its atoms, the probability that these atoms are arranged in a certain order. What is important is the energy of the chemical bonds. The organism takes in food and burns it. It separates and binds atoms and molecules. Work, with a correlative degradation of energy, is produced at the expense of the energy of the chemical bonds. The organism is unable to make use of energy *in abstracto;* it has to perform oxidoreductions. The energy of light allows the plant to separate hydrogen ions from the molecule of water. When light meets atoms, work is produced and energy is degraded. But, according to some physicists I have consulted, it does not seem sound to state that the plant that uses light as its source of energy feeds on the negative entropy of light.

The same seems to be true for the energy of the chemical bond. Unless work is produced, one cannot speak of free energy and of its entropic component. When, as a result of a chemical reaction, the energy of a chemical bond of food is utilized, heat is produced and a part of the energy degraded. In the original chemical bond, one part is available for work, and the other is potential entropy. But energy of high grade, such as the energy of light or of a chemical bond, cannot be subdivided into positive and negative entropy.

Negentropy is a grade of energy. Orderliness is a probability. The organism does not handle concepts of grade or logarithms of probabilities. The organism handles atoms or molecules and the energy of light or of chemical bonds. Nevertheless, some of the physicists I have consulted decided that Schrödinger's formula was perfectly acceptable, whereas others claimed that it did not make sense at all. A general agreement was reached only on one point. If fed with pellets of negative entropy, as positive as negative entropy might be, even a physicist would succumb.

REFERENCES

Brillouin, L. (1956). *Science and Information Theory.* Academic Press, New York.

Klotz, I. M. (1957). *Some Principles of Energetics in Biochemical Reactions.* Academic Press, New York.

Linschitz, H. (1953). The information content of a bacterial cell. In *Essays on the Use of Information Theory in Biology*, edited by H. Quastler, pp. 251–262. University of Illinois Press, Urbana.

Prigogine, I. (1955). *Introduction to Thermodynamics of Irreversible Processes.* Charles C Thomas, Springfield, Ill.

Schrödinger, E. (1944). *What Is Life? The Physical Aspect of the Living Cell.* University Press, Cambridge.

Wiener, N. (1958). *Cybernetics.* Hermann, Paris.

VII. CONCLUSION

We have learned that the very basis of biological order, of specificity and diversity, is a sequence of a few small molecules. We have learned that nucleic acid, considered on the time scale of the organism, is the stable, permanent structure responsible for the *specificity* and for the *reproduction of specificity*. But, considered on the time scale of the world, nucleic acid is the varying structure responsible for mutations and evolution.

Stability and variability reside in the same structure. This dual function of the genetic material is one of the important aspects of life.

Nucleic acid is the blueprint for the synthesis of specific proteins, which in turn are the catalysts for the synthesis of essential metabolites. Nucleic acids and enzymes are, from a functional point of view, complementary macromolecules in the sense that one cannot be produced without the other.

The organism, or the cell, is a complex molecular society in which macromolecules and groups of macromolecules are interacting. The functioning of each enzyme or group of enzymes, so as their synthesis, is controlled by the product of their activity, or better by the needs of the organism. Each group possesses its own regulatory system. All the groups and all the various regulating systems interact.

As a result of evolution, an elaborate system of a feedback mechanism has developed. The functioning of the organism reflects the high degree of coupling between regulating genes, operator genes, structural genes, repressors, enzymes, and metabolism. The normal cell is a structural and functional system of order, in which all macromolecules are interdependent units.

The living organism is an integrated system of macromolecular structures and functions able to reproduce its kind. Waves and particles are the complementary aspects of the atom. Structures and functions are the complementary aspects of the organism. Separated from its context — that is, extracted from the cell — any structure, either a nucleic acid or a protein, is just an organic molecule. Such a thing as living substance or living matter does not exist. Life can only be the appanage of the organism as a whole. Only organisms are alive.

The upsurge of molecular diseases, whether cellular, subviral, or viral, is apparently the consequence of a molecular tendency toward an escape from cellular control, toward autonomy.

The study of viruses has revealed the existence of sequential viral functions controlling the autonomous reproduction of the viral genetic material and the synthesis of viral proteins. These viral functions may be submitted to specific viral repressors.

The genetic material of a virus is sometimes under the control of the regulating mechanisms of the host. The genes of the host cell are sometimes under the control of the virus. The pathological order is dual, structural and functional, just as the normal order is. Normal and pathological entities may undergo structural recombination and exhibit functional interchanges. The story of the cell/virus system is the story of the quadruple interactions between two different types of dual order.

*
* *

In a complex organized system, the units are necessarily interacting. Any one of us, as a human being, has to visualize himself as a person, as an independent unit, and at the same time as a dependent part of a community, as part of a whole. During three weeks, I had the privilege and pleasure to be part of M.I.T. I have discovered something which I already somehow suspected, namely, that M.I.T., just like a living being, is an integrated system of structures and functions. As I am a physician, and as I am interested in disease, I have tried to detect some sign of a pathological process. But so far as I can see, M.I.T. is perfectly healthy. This is probably because the problem of the induction and repression is solved by some elaborate feedback mechanism, some powerful and efficient repressor-operator system, which no macromolecule can resist. And I should like to express my admiration for this institute, the development of which has been so beautifully conceived by Karl Taylor Compton.